THE TRUTH ABOUT CREDIT

A straightforward, honest approach to repairing, rebuilding and regaining control of your credit.

JACQUELINE WILLCOT

© 2025 WILLCOT FINANCIAL ALL RIGHTS RESERVED.

No part of this book may be reproduced in any form or by any electronic or mechanical means, including information storage and retrieval systems, without written permission from the author, except for the use of brief quotations in a book review.

Published in the US. ISBN 979-8998888205

EQUIFAX, EXPERIAN, TRANSUNION, INNOVIS AND LEXISNEXIS ARE REGISTERED TRADEMARKS OF THEIR RESPECTIVE COMPANIES AND WILLCOT FINANCIAL IS IN NO WAY AFFILIATED WITH THESE COMPANIES.

Disclaimer:

The information provided in this book is for educational and informational purposes only and does not constitute legal advice. While every effort has been made to ensure accuracy, readers are encouraged to consult with a qualified consumer law attorney or legal professional for advice specific to their individual situation. Laws and regulations may vary by state, and legal guidance should always be sought when dealing with complex credit or debt issues.

To my husband, Michael Willcot—

Thank you for being my unwavering support. Like a steady anchor, you've brought calm and clarity through every storm. Your strength, perseverance, and constant encouragement have made all the difference, not only for me, but for our family. Despite every challenge, you've shown up with love, dedication, and time. This book is a reflection of that quiet, consistent support. I couldn't have done this without you.

Contents

Introduction	vii
Common Credit Myths: Debunked	1
Identity Theft and Credit Fraud	5
Credit Freezes and Fraud Alerts	9

Phase One

STEP #1: Order Your Credit Reports	15
STEP #2: Review Your Credit Reports	21
STEP #3: Identifying incorrect Information	25

Phase Two

Overview	35
STEP #1: Disputing Inaccurate or Verified Entries	37
STEP #2: Paying or Settling a Delinquent Debt or Account	57
Options and Strategies for Resolving Credit Entries	65
Phase Two Q&A and Actions Steps	75

Phase Three

STEP #1: Your Credit Score	81
STEP #2: Creating and Acquiring Credit	105
Phase Three - Q&A and Actions Steps	123
About the Author	127
Sample Letters and Affidavits	129
Financial Terms Glossary	147
References	163

Introduction

FINANCIAL STABILITY BEGINS WITH YOU!

"My people are destroyed for lack of knowledge..."
– Hosea 4:6

Congratulations on your decision to take control of your financial future! Your commitment to financial recovery and a positive mindset are the essential keys to achieving your goals. This workbook is designed to guide you step by step through the process of taking back control of your credit. By equipping you with the techniques and knowledge needed to empower you, provide for a stable financial future and improve your credit score.

We live in a world where **good credit is no longer just an option, it's a necessity.** Employers, insurance companies, lenders, and landlords all evaluate your credit before making decisions that affect your job opportunities, insurance rates, and ability to secure housing or loans. Fair or not, corporations believe that a responsible financial history translates to responsible behavior in other areas of life. Whether or not we agree with these beliefs, one thing is certain: maintaining good credit is crucial for current... and future generations.

Introduction

I have seen firsthand how the lack of financial knowledge can lead to hardship. Working as a bankruptcy paralegal for 15 years, I encountered countless individuals who found themselves financially ruined; some due to circumstances beyond their control and others due to financial decisions they simply didn't understand. In both cases, the common factor was *missing* knowledge.

Knowledge is the key to financial protection and success.

For example, did you know that some credit card companies offer insurance that covers your payments if you're unexpectedly laid off? Understanding these types of financial tools can help you safeguard against setbacks while also developing the discipline to **budget, save, and build an emergency fund.** The goal is not just to recover, it's to thrive.

I am the oldest of nine, and at one point, there were *11 of us* crammed into a two-bedroom home. Money was tight, which meant I had to start working at *just 15 years old* to help pay the bills. Like many of us, neither my parents nor I were ever taught the ins and outs of credit. When I got married, my husband had no credit, and my credit score was *a mere 450*. Desperate for a solution, I devoured anything I could find on building and repairing credit. What truly amazed me was realizing how many people feel stuck in life simply because of a lack of information.

I find joy in helping people break free from the burden of financial distress. Watching someone finally understand their credit, gain confidence, and step into financial peace is one of the greatest rewards. I once heard the saying, *"If you find something you love to do and would do it for free, you may have found your purpose."*

Teaching **financial literacy** is my purpose.

I firmly believe in *teaching a person to fish rather than just giving them a fish.* You could hire someone to repair your credit, but what happens five years from now if another financial crisis arises? My goal is to equip you with the knowledge and tools to restore and maintain

Introduction

your credit on your own, so you are never left feeling powerless again. While the idea of tackling this journey alone may feel overwhelming, this workbook will guide and support you every step of the way on your road to being your own best advocate.

"A good name is better than precious ointment."

Ecclesiastes 7:1

In today's world, **credit** is like your *calling card*. It tells a story about your financial character and responsibility. I've experienced both sides; being denied credit and called a "deadbeat," and later being offered exclusive perks and opportunities because of my improved financial standing. I have learned how to restore and maintain my credit, and I know you can too.

There are three essential phases to help you
Repair, Rebuild, and Strengthen Your Credit.

PHASE ONE:
UNDERSTANDING AND DISPUTING
YOUR CREDIT REPORT
REPAIR

You'll begin by establishing direct contact with the three major credit bureaus, learning how to order and read your credit reports, and most importantly, understanding the process of disputing inaccurate information.

Introduction

Phase Two:
Addressing Complex Credit Issues
Rebuild

This phase takes you beyond the basics, guiding you through disputing verified entries, handling major financial events such as bankruptcy, foreclosures, and repossessions, and understanding the pros and cons of paying or settling debts. You'll also explore strategies to remove or resolve these financial obstacles.

Phase Three: Building and Protecting Your Credit
Strengthen Your Credit

In third and final phase, you'll learn how your FICO score is calculated, what raises or lowers it, and how to create and acquire new credit. This phase also provides powerful tools, including dispute letters, fraud letters, Identification Theft affidavits, and step-by-step guidance to help you protect and restore your financial reputation.

Your journey toward financial stability is about more than just improving and correcting your credit profile, it's about reclaiming financial freedom, stability, and peace of mind. Giving you the power to change the course your financial future.

One of the greatest financial secrets is this:
Learning Never Ends

Laws , financial systems and technology are always evolving, which means those who continue to seek knowledge will always have the upper hand. My prayer is that this information provides you with the financial wisdom that has transformed my own life.

Now, let's get started!

Common Credit Myths: Debunked

Myth #1: Checking your own credit report will hurt your score.

Truth:
Checking your own credit report is called a "soft inquiry" and does not affect your credit score in any way. In fact, regularly reviewing your report is a smart way to catch errors early.

Myth #2: You should close old, unused credit cards to boost your score.

Truth:
Closing old accounts can actually hurt your score by reducing your overall available credit and shortening your credit history. If there's no annual fee, it's often better to leave old cards open.

Myth #3: Carrying a balance improves your credit score.

Truth:
Carrying a balance and paying interest does not help your score. What matters is low utilization, which means using less than 30%

of your available credit. Paying your balance in full each month is the best strategy.

Myth #4: Your income is factored into your credit score.

Truth:
Your income is not included in your credit report or your credit score calculation. Lenders may ask about your income when you apply for credit, but it's not part of your score.

Myth #5: Once a collection is paid off, it disappears from your credit report.

Truth:
Paying a collection account doesn't automatically remove it. It can still stay on your report for up to seven years from the original delinquency date, but a paid collection looks better to future lenders than an unpaid one.

Myth #6: Does stating to a collection company that a debt may be yours restart the deletion date of your debt on the credit report?

Truth:
No, simply stating that a debt is yours does not restart the deletion date on your credit report. Under the Fair Credit Reporting Act (FCRA), a collection account can only remain on your credit report for seven years from the date of the original delinquency not from when you acknowledge it or speak to a debt collector.
This date is known as the Date of First Delinquency (DOFD), which is when you first missed a payment with the original creditor and never brought the account current. Debt collectors cannot legally change or "re-age" this date just because you admitted the debt or made a payment unless that new delinquency is tied to a new credit obligation (e.g., a new signed agreement).

However, making a payment or entering into a new agreement with the collector can:

Restart the statute of limitations (how long they can sue you, depending on your state law)

Appear as new activity on your report—but the seven-year deletion clock still goes back to the original delinquency

Myth #7: Once I have late payments, charge-offs, or collections on my credit report, it's almost impossible to have a good credit score unless I hire an expensive credit repair company.

Truth:
No, that's a common credit myth. While late payments, charge-offs, and collections can hurt your credit score, it is absolutely possible to rebuild without hiring an expensive credit repair company. You can start by disputing any inaccurate items on your credit report, paying down credit card balances, and making all future payments on time. After a period of consistent on-time payments, older late payments have less impact on your score compared to recent or current ones. Adding positive credit history, such as a secured credit card or becoming an authorized user, can also help improve your score over time. Rebuilding takes consistency, not costly services.

Myth #8

I have old addresses listed on my credit reports. If I remove these addresses, will the negative or delinquent accounts associated with them also be removed when I dispute them?

Truth:
No, removing an old address from your credit report does not automatically delete any delinquent accounts or negative entries that may be tied to that address. Credit reporting agencies do not link the

THE TRUTH ABOUT CREDIT

validity of an account to a particular address. Instead, they verify account information based on your name, Social Security number, and other identifying details.

That said, some credit repair strategies involve removing outdated or incorrect personal information including addresses to help streamline disputes or highlight inconsistencies in how accounts are reported. While this may support your overall credit cleanup efforts, it will not by itself cause negative accounts to be deleted.

To remove delinquent entries, you must dispute each account directly, providing evidence or a valid reason for removal.

Identity Theft and Credit Fraud

Identity theft is one of the fastest-growing crimes in the world today and it can devastate your credit, if you're not prepared. According to the Federal Trade Commission (FTC), nearly 1.4 million identity theft cases were reported in 2021 alone. That's more than one every 25 seconds. Protecting your credit is not just smart, it's essential.

When someone steals your personal information, such as your Social Security number, date of birth, or credit card number, they can open new accounts, run up debts, and leave you with the damage. These fraudulent activities can destroy your credit score, making it harder for you to qualify for loans, apartments, or even jobs.

Warning Signs of Identity Theft:

- Accounts or credit cards you didn't open appear on your credit report.
- You receive bills for services or purchases you don't recognize.
- Debt collectors contact you about debts that aren't yours.
- You see unfamiliar inquiries from companies you haven't applied with.

- You stop receiving your regular bills or financial mail (which could mean someone changed your address).

How to Protect Yourself:

- **Check your credit reports regularly.** Review your reports from all four major bureaus (Experian, Equifax, TransUnion and Innovis) at least once a year—or more often if you suspect fraud. Look for any accounts or activity you don't recognize.
- **Set up alerts.** Many banks and credit card companies offer free alerts for suspicious activity, large transactions, or account changes.
- **Freeze your credit.** A credit freeze restricts access to your credit reports, making it harder for identity thieves to open new accounts in your name. Freezing your credit is free, and you can temporarily lift the freeze whenever you apply for legitimate credit.
- **Use strong passwords and protect your personal information.** Never share your Social Security number, account numbers, or login details unless absolutely necessary, and only with trusted sources.
- **Report suspicious activity immediately.** If you spot unauthorized activity, file a report with the Federal Trade Commission at IdentityTheft.gov, contact the credit bureaus to place a fraud alert on your file, and notify any affected companies.

Remember:

Catching identity theft early is the key to minimizing the damage. The sooner you spot the problem, the faster you can take action and protect your financial future.

Taking simple, proactive steps today can save you from major headaches tomorrow. You've worked too hard to build your credit, so make sure you protect it with the same care and attention!

Credit Freezes and Fraud Alerts

In today's world, protecting your credit isn't just smart, it's necessary. Many consumers don't realize these protections exist or how simple they are to use. Knowing how to use them can give you a strong advantage in protecting your financial future.

What Is a Credit Freeze?

A **credit freeze**, also known as a **security freeze**, restricts access to your credit file.

When your credit is frozen, lenders and other companies cannot pull your credit report to approve new credit applications unless you lift the freeze.

This makes it much harder for identity thieves to open new accounts in your name without your knowledge.

Thanks to federal law changes in 2018, **credit freezes are now free** for all consumers. You can place, lift, or remove a freeze at any time, at no cost with each of the four major credit bureaus (Experian, Equifax, TransUnion, and Innovis).

Key Points About Credit Freezes:

- Free to place and remove.
- Does not affect your existing credit cards, loans, or accounts.
- Does not impact your credit score.
- Can be temporarily lifted when you need to apply for credit.
- Must be placed separately with each bureau.

When to Use a Credit Freeze:

If you believe your personal information has been exposed, or you simply want to add an extra layer of security to your financial life, freezing your credit is one of the strongest steps you can take.

What Is a Fraud Alert?

A **fraud alert** is a notice placed on your credit report that warns lenders to take extra steps to verify your identity before opening a new account.

Unlike a credit freeze, a fraud alert does not block access to your credit file completely; it simply adds a layer of caution.

There are two types of fraud alerts:

- **Initial Fraud Alert:** Lasts for one year and is ideal if you suspect you've been exposed to identity theft.
- **Extended Fraud Alert:** Lasts for seven years and is available if you have confirmed you are a victim of identity theft and file an identity theft report with the FTC

Key Points About Fraud Alerts:

- Free to place.
- Alerts lenders to verify your identity before approving credit.

Credit Freezes and Fraud Alerts

- Easier to apply for new credit compared to a freeze; you won't have to lift anything.
- Requesting a fraud alert with one credit bureau automatically notifies the other two.

When to Use a Fraud Alert:

If you're concerned but not certain your information has been compromised, or if you simply want lenders to take extra steps before approving new accounts, a fraud alert can provide extra peace of mind.

Phase One

In This Section, You'll Learn How To:

REPAIR

UNDERSTAND AND DISPUTE YOUR CREDIT REPORT

- Order Your Personal Credit Reports
- Read and Understand Your Credit Reports
- Identify and Dispute Incorrect Information

STEP #1: Order Your Credit Reports

Under the Fair Credit Reporting Act (FCRA), you are entitled to receive one free credit report per calendar year from each of the four major credit bureaus: Experian®, Equifax®-CSC, TransUnion®, and Innovis®. It's important to note that these bureaus are not government agencies; they are privately owned companies. Contrary to what some may believe, these companies do not store your personal data in their own databases. Instead, they pull your information from LexisNexis®, a data and analytics company that compiles personal and financial records.

In certain situations, you may be eligible to receive additional free reports. If you are unemployed and seeking employment within the next 60 days, receiving government assistance, or have inaccurate information on your report due to fraud, you can request free copies directly from the credit bureaus. Additionally, federal law grants everyone access to a free report through www.AnnualCreditReport.com or by calling 877-322-8228.

It is crucial to obtain your credit report from all four bureaus to ensure accuracy. Not all vendors report to every bureau as most companies only have memberships with one or two, meaning your credit file may vary between reports. By reviewing all four, you can catch discrepancies and address potential errors.

Many credit card companies, such as Discover, Citi, and Bank of America, provide FICO scores directly within your account dashboard. You can also access your credit score and report by visiting the credit bureaus' official websites.

Don't Wait! Get Started Today by ordering your credit reports. If you do not have internet access, you can request your reports by mail. Be sure to include proof of identification, such as a copy of your driver's license or Social Security card, to avoid delays in processing.

CREDIT BUREAUS

EQUIFAX CREDIT INFORMATION SERVICES, INC.
P.O. BOX 740241, Atlanta, GA 30374
To Order Report: 1.800.685.1111
To Report Fraud: 1.800.525.6285
WWW.EQUIFAX.COM

EXPERIAN NATIONAL CONSUMER ASSISTANCE CENTER
P.O. BOX 2002, ALLEN, TX 75013
To Order Report: 1.888.397.3742
To Report Fraud: 1.888.397.3742
WWW.EXPERIAN.COM

TRANSUNION, LLC.
CONSUMER DISCLOSURE CENTER
P.O. BOX 1000, CHESTER, PA 19022
To Order Report: 1.800.888.4213
To Report Fraud: 1.800.916.8800
WWW.TRANSUNION.COM

STEP #1: Order Your Credit Reports

INNOVIS
P.O. BOX 530088, Atlanta, Ga 30353-0088
To Order Report: 1-800-540-2505
To Report Fraud: 1-866-712-0021
INNOVIS.COM

LEXISNEXIS
P.O. BOX 105108, Atlanta, Ga 30348-5108
To Order Report: 1-888-497-0011
CONSUMER.RISK.LEXISNEXIS.COM/REQUEST
To Report Fraud: 1-200-456-1244
CONSUMER.RISK.LEXISNEXIS.COM

While the major credit bureaus are well-known, LexisNexis is a bit of an outlier. So knowing who they are and what they do will serve you well when reviewing your credit information.

LexisNexis is a huge player in the credit reporting agency that is utilized by insurance companies, lenders, and public officials such as the police. They maintain incredible detailed records of your life. You may be surprised by the extent of the information it holds, much of which is shared openly, often without your awareness. In fact, it is a primary source of comprehensive data for the other four credit bureaus.

So, what exactly is on this report? It's far more extensive than most people realize. It includes every house you've ever lived in, the building materials of your home, your HVAC system, your HOA details, even the title company used for your home loan. It also lists the interest rate you paid and the lenders who provided your mortgage. Beyond that, it includes details of every vehicle you've ever owned, down to the VIN number, along with all insurance policies related to those vehicles.

It also records every ticket you've ever received, ranging from speeding violations to misdemeanors and felonies. The report contains every email address, phone number, and address you've ever had, even if you only resided at a particular address for a brief period. It includes details of every license you've held, as well as any that have been revoked. Additionally, it stores public records such as judgments, bankruptcies, and other legal information indefinitely. While a bankruptcy may remain on your Experian, Equifax, TransUnion, and Innovis reports for 7 to 10 years, it will stay on your LexisNexis report permanently.

The permanence of LexisNexis is quite concerning. For instance, if you've had a judgment or tax lien in the past, it could still appear 30 years later when lenders check your LexisNexis report. The alarming part? If you've disputed information with traditional credit bureaus like TransUnion or Equifax, they often verify it through LexisNexis. This means inaccurate or outdated information could still be impacting your creditworthiness, as it remains on your LexisNexis report.

The LexisNexis report can be overwhelming, often exceeding 300 pages, providing a detailed account of your entire life's history. It is a deeply intrusive look into your personal information. The most alarming part is that this data is accessible to anyone, including lenders, credit providers, and even government officials. A long-forgotten criminal record from decades ago could resurface, impacting your ability to secure credit.

LexisNexis data is influencing various aspects of life, including insurance, financing, and even merchant accounts or business credit. This occurs because LexisNexis gathers information from a broad range of sources: government databases, county records, credit agencies, and third-party data providers. In fact, it has agreements with major financial institutions that enable them to share your information across various platforms.

While obtaining car insurance, I was informed by the insurance representative that my monthly premium would be higher than the original quote due to an at-fault accident listed on my record. I

STEP #1: Order Your Credit Reports

immediately explained that the accident was not my fault; I was rear-ended by another driver. Despite providing this information, I was told that LexisNexis was reporting the incident as an at-fault accident on my file.

Because of this inaccurate reporting, I was forced to pay an additional $70 per month for my car insurance. This false designation not only increased my financial burden but also highlights the serious impact that errors on third-party databases like LexisNexis can have on consumers. It is deeply frustrating to be penalized for an event where I was the victim, not the party at fault. Correcting such misinformation is critical to ensuring fair treatment and accurate assessment by insurance companies.

So, what can you do about it? The first step is to get a free copy of your LexisNexis report. You can easily access it by searching online, filling out a brief form, and requesting your report. Once you receive it, carefully go through it and highlight any negative or inaccurate items. The next step is to write a letter disputing these items directly with LexisNexis. It's important to note that you don't need to provide proof in your first dispute. Simply highlight the errors and explain why they're inaccurate. Once submitted, you should expect a response within 30 days. Most people don't even realize that LexisNexis reports can be disputed, and nearly 90% of disputes lead to the removal of inaccurate data. The odds are in your favor.

Many people try to freeze their reports to prevent the bureaus from accessing and posting information to their credit report. I've seen individuals freeze their accounts, at no cost, effectively stopping late payments from being added to the 4 credit bureaus.

When you freeze your LexisNexis report, you restrict access to your data. This means that businesses, lenders, or anyone else who typically uses LexisNexis for background checks (like for credit, insurance, or employment) will not be able to access your information. Freezing your report helps prevent new accounts from being opened in your name and protects against identity theft. However, it doesn't remove or clean up existing information, it simply blocks access to it.

However, the primary goal isn't to freeze your LexisNexis data, but to clean it up. By doing so, you can secure better terms when applying for credit, insurance, or loans, as you'll have control over what lenders see about you. When lenders aren't aware that you know about their hidden data sources, you can use this knowledge legally and ethically to your advantage. The goal is to ensure your LexisNexis report contains accurate and favorable information that improves your chances of approval.

Don't wait… take action today. Get your free LexisNexis report, review it carefully, and start disputing any inaccurate data. By doing this, you'll take control of your financial future and improve your chances of securing favorable terms, whether it's for a loan, credit card, insurance, or business financing.

LexisNexis maintains both FCRA-regulated data and non-FCRA-regulated data. Non-FCRA-regulated data will be information used by the credit bureaus such as public records, extension of credit, insurance, or employment. FCRA-regulated data refers to any personal or financial information about a consumer that is used to make decisions about things like credit, employment, insurance, housing, or other eligibility matters.

STEP #2: Review Your Credit Reports

It's crucial to review each section of your credit report carefully for accuracy. Errors or outdated information can negatively affect your credit score and may be removed upon verification. By obtaining a membership with a bureau or a company that hosts credit bureau reports, you can personally monitor your own credit reports without paying a monthly fee to a third party. Regularly reviewing your reports helps ensure that all information is accurate and up-to-date, contributing to a more reliable assessment of your creditworthiness. Each report should indicate the following:

Personal Information:

- Names (including alias), address (present and past), and employer (present and past)
- Social Security Number

Account Information:

- Name of creditor reporting to the bureau
- Account number for the account being reported to the bureau

- Address of the creditor
- Account information includes the type of account (revolving, collection, open, etc.), date placed for collection, and the estimated date that this item is to be removed. (This date is computed from the last delinquent date for the consumer debt; 7 years for consumer debt, 10 years for BK/foreclosure. Often this date is earlier than the legal date of removal.

Additional Information Included:

1. Balance owed
2. Date the account was updated
3. The original amount
4. The original creditor (if reported by a collection agency)
5. Pay status (current, charge-off, collection, etc.)
6. Account Type (revolving, open, closed)
7. Terms of the credit originally extended (60 months, etc.)
8. Responsibility (who's account is it, individual or joint)
9. Monthly payment amount
10. Current status of the payments (never late, collection, closed, etc.)
11. Account history
12. Last date the creditor reported to the bureau
13. Comments section for the creditor
14. Final statement

CREDIT REPORT
Report Date: 03/14/2025

PERSONAL INFORMATION

Name: John A. Smith
Address: 123 Main Street, Anytown, ST 12345

Social Security Number: XXX-XX-123
Date of Birth: 01/15/1985

ACCOUNT INFORMATION

Creditor	Account Type	Balance	Payments Status	Last Reported
First National Bank	Credit Card	$2,450	Current	03/01/2025
City Finance	Auto Loan	$12,560	90 Days Late	02/15/2025
Home Owner Mortgage	Mortgage	$185,000	Current	02/28/2025

EMPLOYER INFO

Present Employer and Address	Emp. Date	Date Verified
ABC & Associates 987 Main Str, Anytown, Anystate 12345	10/91	12/98
Former Employer and Address ABC, Inc, 456 Second Drive, Anytown, Anystate, 12345		

First City Credit Card

Balance — $4221.00

Credit Limit — $5200.00

Account Number — 99-875981

Monthly Payment — $147.00

Opened — March 20, 2021

Payment History

You've made 100% of payments for this account on time.

Account Status — Open

Type — –

First City Credit Card
P.O. Box 22354
Carterville, OH 74056

STEP #3: Identifying incorrect Information

It's essential to thoroughly review your credit report, as you may find incorrect or unfamiliar information. It's not uncommon to spot inaccuracies, so be sure to highlight any accounts that seem wrong or don't belong to you. If you were to hire a credit repair company, their primary task would be to dispute any negative information, and they would do so consistently, disputing as much as possible and as often as possible. However, keep in mind that there is no guarantee with their credit repair tactics. There's about a 50/50 chance that the negative entry will be removed, and just as likely that it could reappear in the future.

Too many credit repair agency clients experience the joy of a credit report that has deleted entries only to find them to reappear months later. Why is this? Under the Fair Credit Reporting Act (FCRA), a creditor or credit bureau typically has **30 days** to investigate a disputed entry on your credit report. Once you file a dispute, the credit reporting agency must complete its investigation and provide a response within this 30-day period. If the creditor cannot verify the information within that time, the entry must be removed from your report. However, be aware that if the creditor provides a response after the 30-day period, the disputed item could be added back to your credit report.

Tip: The credit report will list the last time that a creditor has updated their entry on your credit report. If you find that it's has been years since a creditor updated their entry, there is a great chance that they will not respond to your dispute. They may have sold the debt or went out of business.

This actually happened to me. I couldn't afford my car payments, so I returned the car to the dealership. Because of this, a voluntary repossession was placed on my credit reports. The car company went out of business. When I saw that the balance on my credit report was much higher than what I originally paid for the car, I disputed it. Since the company was no longer in business to confirm the information, the entire entry was removed from all of my credit reports.

Let's say your report lists a foreclosure on your property, but you still live there. In that case, the report should show that the foreclosure was initiated but not completed. There's a clear distinction between a foreclosure being initiated and one that has been finalized, and this difference can directly impact your FICO score.

The Fair Credit Reporting Act (FCRA) is in place to guarantee that all the information on your credit report is **accurate, up-to-date, and verifiable.** It's crucial to carefully review your credit reports to confirm that every detail is correct and that no incorrect or unauthorized information has been mistakenly linked to your report. Errors occur more often than you might expect, especially if you have a common name like Mary Miller or if you have a generational suffix such as Jr. or Sr. attached to your name. Mistakes like these can impact your credit history and should be addressed immediately.

The Fair Credit Reporting Act (FCRA) is a federal law that promotes the accuracy, fairness, and privacy of information in consumer credit reports. It establishes guidelines for how credit

STEP #3: Identifying incorrect Information

reporting agencies must collect, report, and use consumer data. The law ensures that consumers have the right to dispute incorrect or incomplete information on their credit reports and that credit bureaus must investigate any disputes within a set period. The FCRA also limits who can access your credit report and requires that your personal data is protected from misuse. According to the Federal Trade Commission (FTC), about 1 in 5 people (or 20%) have an error on at least one of their credit reports.

Another example, if your report incorrectly states that you were 90 days late on a payment, but you have documentation proving you were only 30 days late, you have the right to challenge this discrepancy. Under the Fair Credit Reporting Act (FCRA), credit bureaus, including Experian, TransUnion, CSC-Equifax, and Innovis, are legally obligated to report **only accurate and verifiable information.**

PHASE ONE - Q&A AND ACTIONS STEPS

Q&A	QUESTIONS	ANSWER
1	Under the Fair Credit Reporting Act (FCRA), how many free credit reports are you entitled to receive per year from each of the major credit bureaus, and under what circumstances can you request additional report?	Under the FCRA, you are entitled to receive one free credit report per calendar year from each of the four major credit bureaus: Experian, Equifax-CSL TransUnion, and Innovis Additional free reports may be requested if you are unemployed and seeking employment within the next 60 days, receiving government assistance, or have Inaccurate information on your report due to fraud. Additionally, federal law grants everyone access to a free report through www.AnnualCreditReport.com or by calling 877-322-8228.
2	Why is it important to obtain your credit reports from all four major credit bureaus Instead of just one?	Not all vendors report to every credit bureau. Most companies only have memberships with one or two bureaus, meaning your credit file may vary between reports. By reviewing all four, you can catch discrepancies, ensure all Information is accurate, and address any errors that could impact your creditworthiness.
3	What role does LexisNexis play in the credit reporting system, and why is it Important to review your LexisNexis report?	LexisNexis is a data and analytics company that compiles personal and financial records, which are then used by the four major credit bureaus. It contains detailed information beyond standard credit reports, Including past addresses, vehicle ownership, legal records, and even past Insurance policies. Reviewing your LexisNexis report is important because Inaccurate or outdated Information on it can influence lending decisions, Insurance rates, and even background checks. Disputing errors on this report can help improve your overall financial profile.
4	What steps can you take if you find Inaccurate Information on your credit report?	If you find inaccurate information, you should file a dispute with the credit bureau reporting the error. This can be done online, by mail, or by phone. The bureau has 30 days to investigate and either correct or remove the Incorrect Information if it cannot be verified. Additionally, you may need to contact the creditor reporting the inaccurate data to ensure it is updated correctly.
5	How does freezing your LexisNexis report Impact your credit and financial transactions?	Freezing your LexisNexis report restricts access to your personal and financial data, preventing lenders, Insurers, and other entities from retrieving information without your authorization. This can help protect against identity theft and prevent new accounts from being opened in your name. However, It does not remove or correct Inaccurate data-paly a dispute can achieve that.

NOTES

Phase Two

In This Section, You'll Learn How To:

REBUILD

ADDRESS COMPLEX CREDIT ISSUES

- Challenge Confirmed Fraudulent Entries
- Paying or Settling Your Debt and Accounts
- Options Regarding Bankruptcies, Foreclosures, Student Loans
- and MUCH MORE!

Overview

You should now have ordered your credit reports, reviewed each entry to ensure its accuracy, and disputed any entries that have proven not to be 100% accurate per FCRA standards.

Now that Phase One is complete, we will move on to Phase Two. This phase will focus on what to do with the negative entries that were verified by the creditor as being accurate with the credit reporting bureaus. Let's get to it…

STEP #1: Disputing Inaccurate or Verified Entries

This workbook is designed to provide you with accurate, reliable information about credit repair. Unlike other resources that promise quick fixes but leave you worse off when disputed items reappear, this guide focuses on the real laws and regulations that credit repair companies use to successfully remove negative items from your credit report. You'll learn about the legal frameworks that ensure lasting results, so you can improve your credit with confidence.

In contrast to other approaches, which often involve credit repair companies waiting for 60 days to dispute items in the hopes that creditors won't respond, this guide shows you how to challenge the validity of disputed entries right from the start. Creditors may claim an account is yours, but you can contest it if there's fraudulent activity, missing documentation, or false information. This workbook helps you understand the specific situations where you can legally challenge and remove inaccuracies, empowering you to take control of your credit report effectively.

Your Legal Rights

Under this law **15 U.S. Code § 1692g relating to deleting collections**, debt collectors must **notify the consumer of their rights** and provide specific information about the debt, including the amount owed, the creditor's name, and instructions on how to dispute the debt. If the consumer disputes the debt, the collector is required to **halt collection activities** until they verify the debt.

Regarding deletion of collections, **this law does not directly mandate the deletion of collections from your credit report**, but it provides a framework under which you may be able to remove inaccurate or disputed collection accounts.

Here are some key points under **15 U.S. Code § 1692g** that can help with removing collections:

1. **Validation of Debt**: Under the Fair Debt Collection Practices Act (FDCPA), if a consumer disputes a debt within 30 days of receiving the initial notice from a debt collector, the collector is legally required to provide proper validation before continuing any collection efforts. This validation must include proof that the debt is legitimate and that the collector is authorized to collect it. If the collector cannot validate the debt, they must cease all collection activity and may not continue to report the debt to credit bureaus. Any existing reporting related to that debt should be removed from the consumer's credit reports.
2. **Disputing a Debt**: If a collection account is being inaccurately reported—for example, showing the wrong balance, dates, or if the debt doesn't belong to the consumer—it can be disputed under the Fair Credit Reporting Act (FCRA). Consumers may file disputes with both the credit bureaus and the debt collector. If the debt collector fails to validate the debt in response to the dispute, they are

STEP #1: Disputing Inaccurate or Verified Entries

generally required to delete the collection account from the credit report, as unverified or inaccurate information cannot remain.

3. **Improper Collection Practices**: Debt collectors who violate the rules outlined in the FDCPA, such as harassing the consumer, making false threats, failing to validate the debt, or disclosing the debt to third parties without consent, are engaging in illegal practices. These violations not only expose the collector to legal consequences, but may also form a basis for demanding the removal of the collection account from credit reports. Consumers have the right to file complaints with the Consumer Financial Protection Bureau (CFPB), sue for damages, and request account deletion in certain situations.

4. **Failure to Notify Before Reporting**: The FDCPA also requires that debt collectors send a written notice of the debt within five days of their first contact with a consumer. This notice must inform the consumer of their right to dispute the debt. If a debt is reported to the credit bureaus before the consumer has received this notice, or before they've been given a chance to respond, it may constitute a procedural violation. In such cases, the collection account may be subject to removal due to the collector's failure to follow required legal steps.

Can collections be deleted under this law?

Yes, but primarily if the debt collector fails to follow the legal procedures required under the Fair Debt Collection Practices Act (FDCPA). For example, if they do not provide proper validation of the debt after it's disputed, report the debt to credit bureaus before notifying the consumer in writing, or engage in illegal practices such as harassment or making false threats, these actions can be considered when determining whether deletion is warranted. In such cases, the consumer may have grounds to request that the collection account be removed from their credit report, either through dispute resolution, legal action, or as part of a settlement.

Steps to Remove Collections under 15 U.S. Code § 1692g:

1. **Send a Debt Validation Letter**: If you are contacted by a collection agency, you have the right under the Fair Debt Collection Practices Act (FDCPA) to send a debt validation letter within 30 days of their initial contact. A debt validation letter is a formal written request that asks the collection agency to provide proof that the debt is legitimate, that they have the legal right to collect it, and that the amount they are attempting to collect is accurate. This may include documentation such as the original account agreement, a breakdown of the balance, and evidence that the debt has been assigned or sold to them. Once your request is received, the debt collector must pause all collection efforts, including calls, letters, and credit reporting, until they have provided adequate validation. If they fail to validate the debt, they are legally prohibited from continuing collection activity, and you can request that the collection account be removed from your credit report due to their non-compliance with federal law.

2. **Dispute with the Credit Bureaus**: If the debt collector does not validate the debt or provides incomplete or inaccurate information, such as the wrong amount, missing documentation, or failure to show their authority to collect, you can file a dispute with the credit bureaus (Experian, Equifax, TransUnion and Innovis). For example, if the collector sends a vague statement or fails to link the debt to your name with supporting records, that may be considered insufficient validation. Once you dispute the debt, the credit bureaus are required to investigate by contacting the

STEP #1: Disputing Inaccurate or Verified Entries

collector. If the collector cannot provide proper verification during the investigation, the credit bureaus are legally required to remove the collection account from your credit report.

3. **Contact the Collector**: If you believe the debt is erroneous, for example, if it's not yours, has been paid, was already settled, or is reported with incorrect details, you have the right to contact the original creditor or the debt collector directly to request a correction or removal. This is often done in writing to create a paper trail. You can explain the specific inaccuracies and request that they investigate the matter internally. In some cases, particularly when the error is clear or well-documented, the creditor or collector may agree to remove the account or update it to reflect the correct status (such as "paid," "settled," or "disputed"). Always request written confirmation of any agreed changes, and follow up by sending that documentation to the credit bureaus to ensure your credit report is updated accordingly.

15 U.S. Code § 1692g is part of the **Fair Debt Collection Practices Act (FDCPA)**, a federal law designed to protect consumers from unfair debt collection practices. If collections are not properly validated or if there are violations of the law, you can potentially have them removed from your credit report. However, the law itself doesn't directly mandate deletion. Rather, it provides a process for disputing and validating debts, which can lead to the removal of inaccurate collections.

Here are some examples of debt collectors failing to provide proper validation of the debt, not following the correct procedures required by law, or using illegal practices under the Fair Debt Collection Practices Act (FDCPA), such as threatening legal action they have no intention of taking, contacting you at inconvenient hours, or disclosing your debt to third parties without your consent, all of which violate your rights and can provide grounds for disputing the debt or seeking legal recourse.

1. Failure to Provide Debt Validation

Under **15 U.S. Code § 1692g(a)**, when a consumer receives a debt collection notice, the collector must provide certain information, including:

- The amount of the debt.
- The name of the creditor to whom the debt is owed.
- A notice that the consumer has the right to dispute the debt within 30 days of receiving the notice.

Example:

- A debt collector contacts a consumer about a debt but does not provide the required information, such as the creditor's name or the amount owed.
- If the consumer requests validation of the debt, and the collector does not provide proper documentation (such as a statement of the debt, contract, or proof of ownership), the debt collector has violated the FDCPA.
- **Consequence**: The debt cannot be legally collected or reported, and if reported on the consumer's credit report, it could be removed.

Follow-Up Steps: If the Collector Fails to Validate the Debt

- Wait 30–45 days after sending the letter (certified mail with return receipt recommended).
- If the collector does not respond, or responds without proper validation:
- Gather your proof of the letter sent (copy + mail receipt)
- Note the lack of meaningful response or continued collection activity

STEP #1: Disputing Inaccurate or Verified Entries

- File a dispute with the credit bureaus (Experian, Equifax, TransUnion and Innovis):
- Include a copy of your original validation letter
- Include proof of mailing
- Explain that the collector failed to validate the debt and should not be reporting it

If the credit bureau cannot verify the debt with the collector, they are legally required to remove the item from your credit report within 30 days.

2. Failure to Stop Collection Activities During Dispute

Under **15 U.S. Code § 1692g(b)**, if a consumer disputes a debt in writing within 30 days of receiving the notice, the debt collector must cease collection activities until they verify the debt. This includes stopping collection calls, reporting the debt, or taking legal action.

Example:

- A consumer receives a debt collection notice and disputes the debt within 30 days. However, the debt collector continues to call or sends further letters attempting to collect the debt, even though the consumer has disputed it.
- **Consequence**: The consumer can file a complaint, and the debt collector must stop collection activities until the debt is validated.

Follow-Up Steps: Failure to Stop Collection Activities During a Dispute

If a debt collector continues to pursue collection, including phone calls, letters, or reporting to the credit bureaus, after you've submitted a debt validation request, they may be violating the Fair Debt Collection Practices Act (FDCPA).

Here's what to do next:

Document Everything

- Keep a copy of your original debt validation letter
- Keep proof of delivery (certified mail receipt or tracking confirmation)
- Log any calls, voicemails, texts, or emails from the collector after your dispute was sent
- Save any updated credit reports showing the debt still being reported

Send a Cease-and-Desist or Follow-Up Letter

If the collector continues to contact you or report the debt without validating it, send a second letter demanding they stop all collection activities. Reiterate that the debt is in dispute and they are violating federal law by continuing to pursue it.

File Complaints

If the collector still does not comply, file a complaint with:

- The Consumer Financial Protection Bureau (CFPB): consumerfinance.gov/complaint
- Your state attorney general's office
- The Federal Trade Commission (FTC)

- Consider Legal Action
- You may also contact a consumer rights attorney. Under the FDCPA, you can sue a collector for damages—up to $1,000 plus legal fees—for continuing to collect without validating the debt or violating other provisions of the law.

STEP #1: Disputing Inaccurate or Verified Entries

3. Reporting Debt After It Has Been Disputed

If a debt collector continues to report a disputed debt to the credit bureaus without validating the debt, they are violating the FDCPA. The collection account should not appear on the credit report until it is properly validated.

Example:

- A consumer disputes a debt with a collector but sees that the debt is still being reported on their credit report as unpaid, even though the collector has not provided validation.
- **Consequence:** The consumer can dispute the entry with the credit bureaus and, if the debt is not validated, request that the collection be removed.

Follow-Up Steps for Wrong or Unvalidated Debts Still Being Reported

If you've disputed a debt because it is incorrect or the debt collector failed to validate it, and it still appears on your credit report, take the following steps to escalate the matter:

Gather All Documentation

- Copy of your debt validation request sent to the collector
- Proof of certified mail or delivery receipt
- Any response (or lack of response) from the collector
- Most recent credit report showing the debt is still being reported

File a Formal Dispute with the Credit Bureaus

Contact Experian, Equifax, TransUnion and Innovis, and Include:

- Your original dispute letter
- Proof that you requested validation
- A clear explanation that the debt is unvalidated and should not be reported

Tip: You can mail your dispute or submit it online through each bureau's dispute portal.

Demand Removal Under FCRA and FDCPA

- State that under the Fair Credit Reporting Act (FCRA), unverifiable information must be deleted
- Under the FDCPA, debt collectors cannot continue reporting a debt without proper validation

File a Complaint

- If the bureaus or debt collector continue to report the debt, file formal complaints with:
- Consumer Financial Protection Bureau (CFPB): consumerfinance.gov/complaint
- Federal Trade Commission (FTC)
- Your State Attorney General's Office

Consider Legal Action

If all else fails, consult a consumer law attorney. You may be able to sue the collector or credit bureau for reporting false or unvalidated information, which could result in:

- Monetary damages
- Legal fees covered
- Court-ordered deletion of the debt from your credit report

STEP #1: Disputing Inaccurate or Verified Entries

4. Use of Deceptive or Harassing Practices

The FDCPA prohibits debt collectors from using **harassment, false statements**, or **deceptive practices**. These practices can include lying about the debt, threatening legal action that cannot be taken, or contacting the consumer at inappropriate times.

Examples:

- **Threats of arrest or legal action**: A debt collector threatens to have the consumer arrested or taken to court when they do not have the legal authority or intention to do so.
- **Contacting at unreasonable hours**: Debt collectors repeatedly call or send collection notices early in the morning or late at night, which is prohibited.
- **Misleading statements**: A debt collector falsely tells a consumer that paying a certain amount will settle the debt, but in reality, the consumer still owes more.

Consequence: These deceptive or harassing practices are illegal under the FDCPA. If a consumer experiences these actions, they can report the debt collector to the Federal Trade Commission (FTC) or sue the debt collector for damages, and the collection account could be removed from their credit report.

5. Inaccurate Reporting

Debt collectors are required to report accurate information. If they report incorrect details about a debt (such as an incorrect balance, wrong dates, or erroneous account information), it can violate the law.

Example:

- A debt collector reports an incorrect balance on a debt (e.g., the amount is higher than the actual debt), or they report the

debt after the statute of limitations has expired, making the debt appear valid when it is not.
- **Consequence**: The consumer can dispute the inaccurate reporting with the credit bureaus, and the collection account may be removed if the information is not properly verified.

If a debt collector violates the provisions of the **FDCPA**, including failing to provide validation, using illegal practices, or improperly reporting a debt, the consumer may have the right to:

1. **Dispute the Debt**: Contact the credit bureaus to dispute inaccurate or invalid debts.
2. **Sue the Debt Collector**: Consumers may file a lawsuit in state or federal court against the debt collector for damages. The FDCPA allows for damages of up to **$1,000** for statutory violations, plus actual damages (e.g., emotional distress) and attorney fees.
3. **Request Removal of the Debt**: If the debt is found to be invalid or incorrectly reported, it may be removed from the consumer's credit report.

Debt collectors must follow strict procedures under **15 U.S. Code § 1692g** to ensure they validate debts, provide accurate information, and avoid deceptive or harassing practices. If they fail to do so, consumers have legal grounds to dispute or seek removal of collections from their credit report.

Follow-Up Steps if a Debt Collector Reports Inaccurate Information

Debt collectors are required by law to report accurate and truthful information to credit reporting agencies. If they report false or misleading details, such as an inflated balance, incorrect dates, or a debt that's beyond the statute of limitations, you have the right to challenge and correct it.

Identify the Inaccuracy

STEP #1: Disputing Inaccurate or Verified Entries

- Review your credit reports for:
- Wrong balance amounts
- Incorrect account dates (e.g., date opened, last payment)
- Debts reported past the statute of limitations for your state
- Debts that don't belong to you at all

Dispute the Error with the Credit Bureaus

- File a dispute with Experian, Equifax, and TransUnion
- Clearly explain what's wrong and why it's inaccurate
- Include any supporting documentation, such as payment records or correspondence

Notify the Debt Collector

- Send a written notice to the debt collector explaining the error
- Request that they correct the reporting or provide proof that it's accurate
- Send via certified mail and keep copies for your records

Allow Time for Investigation

- Credit bureaus have 30 days to investigate your dispute
- If the collector can't verify the information, they must remove or correct the account

Take Action if the Error Remains

If the incorrect info is not corrected, file complaints with:

- CFPB (consumerfinance.gov)
- FTC
- Your state attorney general

- Consider contacting a consumer protection attorney for possible legal action

Result:

If the collector or bureau fails to verify the disputed information, the inaccurate collection must be corrected or removed from your credit report under the Fair Credit Reporting Act (FCRA).

Confirmed Fraudulent Entry

When dealing with a fraudulent entry, it is imperative to report the fraud to the police first. After receiving a copy of the police report, mail the creditor and credit bureaus a copy of the FRAUD letter enclosed with a copy of the police report. Per the Fair Credit Billing Act (FCBA), the creditor is not allowed to charge you more than $50.00 for the fraudulent charges on your <u>credit card</u>. If a fraudulent charge occurs on a lost or stolen card, the cardholder may not be held responsible for any charges once they report the theft.

The Fair Credit Billing Act (FCBA) protects consumers from unfair billing practices and allows them to dispute errors on their credit card statements. If you spot an error, you can dispute it in writing and withhold payment while it's being investigated. The creditor must respond within 30 days and resolve the issue within two billing cycles. This law ensures you're not held responsible for fraudulent or incorrect charges. You may come across a charge that you don't recognize and decide to call your creditor to ask about it. After confirming that the charge wasn't yours, you dispute it with the creditor. The creditor will temporarily refund the money while they go through their verification process. If the investigation shows the charge wasn't yours, the credit will stay on your account. However, if it turns out you did make the charge, the amount will be deducted from your account.

STEP #1: Disputing Inaccurate or Verified Entries

With the combination of FCRA and FCBA, fraudulent entries cannot continue to be reported on your credit report. If you encounter difficulties or face resistance from the credit bureaus when trying to have these entries removed, hiring an attorney may be a beneficial solution. An attorney specializing in consumer rights or credit law (Consumer Advocate Attorney) can help ensure that your rights are fully protected. They can assist in navigating complex disputes, draft legal letters, and, if necessary, take legal action against the credit bureaus or creditors to force them to correct inaccurate information. In some cases, an attorney may even help you recover damages if the credit bureaus fail to comply with the laws. Some local bar associations offer programs where you can meet with an attorney for a brief consultation, often around 30 minutes, for a small fee, sometimes as low as $20.

Legal Remedies Under the FDCPA: Dispute and Defend with Confidence

We've all encountered persistent collection agencies attempting to collect a debt they either purchased or were hired by a creditor to pursue. Under the **Fair Debt Collection Practices Act (FDCPA)**, creditors and debt collectors must provide written verification of a debt if requested by the consumer. This is called a "**debt validation request**." If the creditor cannot provide sufficient evidence of the debt, such as a signed contract, the debt can be challenged and potentially removed from your credit report.

The Fair Debt Collection Practices Act (FDCPA) is a federal law that protects consumers from abusive debt collection practices. It restricts how debt collectors can contact you, ensuring they do not use unfair or deceptive tactics. The law also gives consumers the right to dispute debts and request verification from debt collectors.

To do this, you should send a certified letter to the creditor requesting proof that the debt is yours. You can ask for various forms of documentation, such as: a signed contract, payment records, or any other evidence that confirms the debt is valid and belongs to you.

If the creditor fails to provide the necessary evidence, you have the right to dispute the debt with the credit bureaus or seek legal remedies. After 30 days, submit a certified copy of the return receipt showing that the creditor received your evidence request, along with a copy of the letter. Request that the disputed entry be deleted from your credit report if the creditor cannot verify the debt. Many debt buyers have little more than your name and Social Security number, making it difficult for them to properly verify the debt. If they are unable to provide adequate proof, the debt may be removed from your credit report.

Tip: We've all encountered persistent creditors who aggressively call to collect on a debt, but the **Fair Debt Collection Practices Act (FDCPA)** forbids creditor harassment. For instance, debt collectors cannot use abusive language, such as profane, obscene, or threatening language when communicating with you.

They are also prohibited from threatening physical harm or violence against you or your property. Additionally, they cannot harass you by making repeated calls, especially at odd hours like late at night or early in the morning, nor can they contact you at work if they know your employer disapproves. Debt collectors cannot lie about the debt, including falsely claiming to be attorneys or government officials, or threatening you with arrest or jail time. They are also prohibited from misleading you about the amount or status of the debt, such as telling you the debt has increased due to illegal fees or interest. Debt collectors cannot contact your friends, family, or coworkers about your debt, except to confirm your location, and they cannot disclose the nature of the debt to others. Furthermore, they cannot threaten to take legal action they have no intention or ability to pursue, nor can they falsely report information to credit bureaus or fail to remove incorrect negative information once the debt is paid or resolved. Debt collectors are also prohibited from impersonating law

STEP #1: Disputing Inaccurate or Verified Entries

enforcement or government agents to intimidate you, as well as from using deceptive tactics, such as offering to "settle" a debt without providing proper details or making you believe you have no legal options.

If debt collectors violate the FDCPA, you may be entitled to various types of remedies. These include **actual damages**, which cover any financial harm caused by the collector's actions, such as lost wages or medical expenses from the stress of harassment. Consumers may also receive **statutory damages**, up to **$1,000**, as set by law, regardless of financial harm. Additionally, if the consumer successfully sues the debt collector, they may be awarded **attorney's fees** and **court costs** to cover legal expenses.

Armed with the knowledge of the Fair Debt Collection Practices Act (FDCPA), I was at a friend's house while she was receiving calls repeatedly from a debt collector. I asked her if I could impersonate her, and she agreed. The debt collector began harassing me, claiming they were going to sue and pressuring me to make a payment immediately. I calmly informed them that, under the FDCPA, they could not threaten me like this. I also told them that, according to the law, I no longer wanted them to contact me about this debt and would be sending a written request to cease all future communication. I made it clear that if they contacted me again, I would sue them for violating the FDCPA. They quickly hung up, realizing they couldn't intimidate me. My friend looked at me with wide eyes, utterly shocked. It was that easy. **When you gain knowledge in any area, you hold the power.**

Identity Theft and Credit Fraud

Identity theft is one of the fastest-growing crimes in the world today, and it can devastate your credit if you're not prepared. According to the Federal Trade Commission (FTC), nearly 1.4 million identity theft cases were reported in 2021 alone. That's more than one every 25 seconds. Protecting your credit is not just smart… it's essential.

When someone steals your personal information, such as your Social Security number, date of birth, or credit card number, they can open new accounts, run up debts, and leave you with the damage. These fraudulent activities can destroy your credit score, making it harder for you to qualify for loans, apartments, or even jobs.

Warning Signs of Identity Theft:

- Accounts or credit cards you didn't open appear on your credit report.
- You receive bills for services or purchases you don't recognize.
- Debt collectors contact you about debts that aren't yours.
- You see unfamiliar inquiries from companies you haven't applied with.
- You stop receiving your regular bills or financial mail (which could mean someone changed your address).

How to Protect Yourself:

- **Check your credit reports regularly.** Review your reports from all three major bureaus (Experian, Equifax, and TransUnion) at least once a year, or more often if you suspect fraud. Look for any accounts or activity you don't recognize.
- **Set up alerts.** Many banks and credit card companies offer free alerts for suspicious activity, large transactions, or account changes.
- **Freeze your credit.** A credit freeze restricts access to your credit reports, making it harder for identity thieves to open new accounts in your name. Freezing your credit is free, and you can temporarily lift the freeze whenever you apply for legitimate credit.
- **Use strong passwords and protect your personal information.** Never share your Social Security number,

STEP #1: Disputing Inaccurate or Verified Entries

account numbers, or login details unless absolutely necessary, and only with trusted sources.
- **Report suspicious activity immediately.** If you spot unauthorized activity, file a report with the Federal Trade Commission at IdentityTheft.gov, contact the credit bureaus to place a fraud alert on your file, and notify any affected companies.

Remember:

Catching identity theft early is the key to minimizing the damage. The sooner you spot the problem, the faster you can take action and protect your financial future.

Taking simple, proactive steps today can save you from major headaches tomorrow. You've worked too hard to build your credit, make sure you protect it with the same care and attention!

False/Untrue Entries

If an entry is inaccurate or false, you'll need documentation to prove that it's not yours or that it's being reported incorrectly. For instance, if the entry claims you were 60 days late three times over the year, having a transaction record showing when the payment cleared from your account can serve as evidence to dispute the claim with the Bureaus. This will help ensure that the entry is corrected. Be sure to send a copy of the dispute letter below.

In all of these cases, remember to **send your letters by certified mail with a return receipt.** If the creditor doesn't respond within 30 days, send a copy of the no response letter to the credit reporting agencies, along with the letter and the return receipt that was mailed to the creditor. This step is essential for disputing the credit reporting agency's claim that the creditor verified the disputed entry. If the creditor was unable to verify it with you, how could they have verified it with the credit bureaus? Sending your letter via certified mail to the credit bureau provides proof that they received it.

I once had a credit bureau send me a letter just three days after receiving my dispute, claiming they had contacted all of my creditors. I was able to demonstrate that it would have been virtually impossible for them to conduct such extensive research and verify all of my disputes in such a short period of time. The timeline simply didn't add up, and this proof helped me challenge the bureau's response.

STEP #2: Paying or Settling a Delinquent Debt or Account

Settling a debt means you negotiate with the creditor or collection agency to pay **less than the total amount owed**, and they agree to consider the debt resolved. While this is a common practice, it's important to fully understand the implications before you make a payment.

Here's the common dilemma: If you're applying for new credit, some lenders may require you to pay off or settle outstanding debts before approving your application. For example, if you owe $100, the collection agency may offer to settle the account for $50. In this case, the creditor agrees to take a smaller amount to close the account.

Although settlements are legal and widely used, it's essential to know how they affect your credit. Some people mistakenly believe that a paid collection is treated the same as an unpaid collection on your FICO score but this is not entirely true. Research and industry data show that a paid or settled collection can still have a negative impact on your credit, but lenders often view resolved debts more favorably than unresolved ones. Plus, newer scoring models like FICO 9 and VantageScore 3.0/4.0 tend to ignore paid collections entirely, which could work in your favor. We will talk more about the Credit scoring systems in phrase three.

That said, before you pay or settle anything, always get written confirmation of the agreement, preferably on the company's letterhead. This written agreement should clearly state the payment amount, the settlement terms, and whether the account will be deleted from your credit report. Never send money until you have this letter in hand. Too many consumers have paid a debt based on a verbal promise, only to find that the creditor did not honor the agreement.

If you have the funds to pay the full amount, ask the creditor or collector, "Do you delete?" Many will agree to remove the account from your credit report if you pay in full; they just want the money. But again, get this agreement in writing first. Your letter should say something like:

Dear [Your Name],
[CREDITOR'S NAME] agrees to delete this debt of $1000.00 from all credit bureaus if paid in full.

And it should always be printed on their official company letterhead.

Another detail many people overlook is that settled debt can be considered **taxable income by the IRS**. If a portion of your debt is forgiven (i.e., you pay $500 of a $1,000 debt), the forgiven amount ($500) may be treated as Cancellation of Debt Income (CODI). If the forgiven amount is $600 or more, the creditor may issue you a Form 1099-C, which you must report on your tax return.

Paying off a delinquent debt is a significant decision, and it's important to approach it strategically. While many consumers believe that simply paying a collection will automatically boost their credit score, that's not always the case. Once an account has reached collection status, the negative impact to your credit has already occurred. Paying it off does not erase the damage, it only updates the account status to paid. Resolving the debt can still be beneficial in the long term, especially when applying for new credit, renting an apartment,

STEP #2: Paying or Settling a Delinquent Debt or Account

or even seeking employment where credit checks may be part of the process.

One of the most critical yet overlooked steps in this process is documentation. It's essential to get every agreement or conversation with a creditor or collection agency in writing. Verbal promises can be easily forgotten or denied, leaving you without proof of what was agreed upon. Always ask for confirmation letters that clearly state the terms of any arrangement, payment acknowledgment, or changes to the account status. These letters should be printed on the company's official letterhead and kept in a safe place for your records. They serve as your only protection if any discrepancies arise later on your credit report.

In addition to written documentation, you should also make it a habit to take detailed notes during every phone call. Record the name of the representative you spoke with, the date and time of the call, and the key points of the discussion. These notes can be incredibly helpful if you need to reference the conversation later, especially if you speak with a different representative in the future. In some cases, multiple representatives may provide conflicting information and have a clear record of who said what can help you resolve any inconsistencies quickly and confidently.

By treating every interaction with a collection agency or creditor like a formal business transaction, you protect yourself from miscommunication, errors, and potential disputes. Good record-keeping can make a significant difference in how smoothly the process goes, and can help you assert your rights if any issues arise. When it comes to managing your credit, preparation and documentation are just as important as the payment itself.

In my 15 years of working with bankruptcy transactions, I have encountered countless individuals who, after paying off debts, whether it be mortgage payments, rental leases, or medical bills, find that the debts still appear as unpaid on their credit reports. One of the most common phrases I hear from them is, "But I paid that!" This situation can be incredibly frustrating, and unfortunately, it's more common than many people realize. There's often a disconnect between what the consumer believes has been settled and how it's reported, which can have a lasting impact on their credit.

Take my dear friend Cindy, for example. She had moved out of her apartment after paying her lease in full and ensuring the apartment was cleaned. However, she neglected to have the management staff conduct a final walk-through and sign off on the move-out paperwork. Months later, she was blindsided with a $1,500 bill for damages and cleaning fees. Cindy had no proof to dispute these charges, no pictures, no video, and no documentation of the apartment's condition, when she moved out. Without that evidence, she was left with nothing to defend herself, and the bill appeared on her credit report as a delinquent collection account. This situation could have been avoided if she had taken the time to request a signed statement or properly documented the apartment's condition on her move-out date.

I've also witnessed cases where individuals had to file for bankruptcy due to a potential foreclosure being filed against their home, even though they had made all of their mortgage payments. In many of these cases, the banks had poor record-keeping systems, which led them to mistakenly file foreclosures on multiple homeowners, many of whom were current with their payments.

These errors in the bank's paperwork resulted in serious consequences for homeowners, including foreclosure proceedings and damaged credit scores, despite their efforts to stay current on their loans.

This highlights how crucial it is for consumers to stay vigilant and document everything, especially in financial transactions where a mistake or oversight can have long-lasting effects.

The moral of these stories is clear: always be proactive and ensure that you have proper documentation for all transactions. If there's a

STEP #2: Paying or Settling a Delinquent Debt or Account

chance that a debt could appear as unpaid on your credit report, take the necessary steps to keep your records in order. Having proof can be the difference between having your debts properly reported and finding yourself dealing with a financial setback you didn't cause.

It's crucial for consumers to stay alert and carefully document every step, particularly in financial transactions where even a small error or oversight can lead to long-term consequences.

THE TAKEAWAY IS SIMPLE:

Always be proactive and make sure you maintain proper documentation for every transaction.

SETTLING THE DEBT

PROS	CONS
Satisfaction of paying the debt.	No dramatic increase in score.
No more debt collection calls.	No cancellation of debt entries.
Debt cannot be sold to a debt collection agency.	

PAYING THE DEBT

PROS	CONS
Satisfaction of paying the debt.	Without a deletion letter, the account will affect your credit score for 7 years.
No more debt collection calls.	
If the account is not in collections or charged off. It may help improve your credit standing.	
Paying Debt with a delete letter can improve your score.	

Options and Strategies for Resolving Credit Entries

Bankruptcy, Foreclosure, Student Loans, Medical Debt, and Liens

Many credit repair companies promise to remove these items. Bankruptcies, foreclosures, and other negative marks on your credit report are governed by specific time limits under the law; bankruptcies and foreclosures remain for 10 years, and tax liens or judgments stay for 7 years. However, a creditor can renew a lien or judgment for an additional 7 years, typically by filing a request through the court process before the original 7-year reporting period expires. If the renewal is granted, the negative item can remain on the credit report for up to 14 years. It is important to understand that accurate, negative items on your report is not supposed to be removed before the legally mandated time period. If you believe an item is incorrect or outdated, the best practice is to dispute it with the credit bureaus, providing supporting evidence of any inaccuracies. Fraudulent or misleading actions, such as submitting false disputes or misrepresenting information, can lead to serious legal consequences. It's crucial to follow legal avenues when managing your credit report to ensure long-term financial health and avoid potential penalties or the reappearance of negative information after a fraudulent removal by a credit repair agent.

Bankruptcy

Bankruptcy can be a beneficial legal tool for reducing your debt liability and providing a fresh financial start. By filing for bankruptcy, you can potentially minimize or eliminate your obligations related to foreclosure, liens, repossessions, lawsuits, and judgments. For example, in a Chapter 7 bankruptcy, unsecured debts such as credit card balances and medical bills may be discharged entirely, meaning you are no longer legally required to pay them. In the case of a foreclosure, bankruptcy may stop the process temporarily (through an automatic stay), allowing you time to reorganize your finances or, in some cases, negotiate a settlement with creditors.

Filing for bankruptcy can have a positive long-term impact on your credit report, though it's important to understand that it doesn't immediately boost your credit score. While bankruptcy remains on your credit report for several years (7 years for Chapter 13 and 10 years for Chapter 7), it can help by clearing a significant portion of your debt. This reduction in debt can improve your debt-to-income ratio, which is a key factor in rebuilding your credit. With your debt balances reduced to zero, your credit score may begin to rise over time.

For example, I've seen someone start with a 350 FICO score before filing for bankruptcy and improve to a 700 score just one year after. Creditors recognize that you no longer have outstanding debt, which shows you are now able to pay them. While each situation is different, filing for bankruptcy can open the door to rebuilding your credit and securing a stronger financial future.

Many bankruptcy attorneys offer free consultations, which can help you understand how filing for bankruptcy can benefit your specific situation and whether it's the right option for reducing your debt liability. They can guide you on how to handle foreclosure, judgments, liens, and repossessions in the context of bankruptcy, helping you make an informed decision based on your financial goals.

Options and Strategies for Resolving Credit Entries

Student Loans

Many of us sought a better path in life and chose to attend college with the goal of achieving that dream. Along the way, we were presented with the option to finance our education through student loans. Unfortunately, many of us were not fully educated on the complexities of debt, especially how compounding interest can quickly grow the amount owed beyond what we originally borrowed. As a result, many student loans have gone into default, making it difficult for graduates to pay them off after finishing school.

There are very few options available to extinguish student loan debt, and many of them come with significant challenges. One of the most difficult options is discharging student loans through bankruptcy. While it is possible in certain circumstances, it is a complex and rare process that requires meeting specific criteria to prove "undue hardship." Even then, it's not a guaranteed outcome.

However, having a federal student loan provides more options and flexibility than a private student loan. Federal loans come with protections such as the ability to rehabilitate loans in default. Through rehabilitation, borrowers can make a series of agreed-upon monthly payments, which **removes the default status from their credit report once completed**. Additionally, borrowers can consolidate federal loans, which may also remove the default status if the consolidation is successful.

Federal student loan borrowers also have access to income-driven repayment plans that adjust payments based on income, as well as the Public Service Loan Forgiveness (PSLF) program, which can forgive the remaining loan balance after meeting certain conditions. These federal options offer a clearer pathway to managing or reducing student loan debt, improving the borrower's financial situation and credit score. Unfortunately, private student loans typically do not offer these same protections, making federal loans a more favorable choice for many borrowers seeking ways to manage or eliminate their debt and improving their credit score.

Property Taxes and IRS Tax Liens

Regarding property tax liens, there are two options that can help alleviate the burden of overdue property taxes. The first option involves organizations or third-party lenders that provide loans using your property as collateral to pay off your outstanding taxes. These companies often offer short-term loans specifically designed to clear property tax debts, allowing you to avoid foreclosure and gain more time to pay off the loan. However, it's important to note that these loans often come with high interest rates and fees, which can add to your financial burden, so it's crucial to review the terms carefully before proceeding.

The second option involves filing for bankruptcy, specifically Chapter 13, which allows you to include past-due property taxes in the repayment plan. Under Chapter 13, you can pay off your overdue taxes over a period of 3 to 5 years, depending on your income and the specifics of your case. This option can prevent foreclosure and provide a structured way to catch up on taxes while still managing other debts. Additionally, filing for bankruptcy may offer the chance to discharge some unsecured debts, improving your overall financial situation and ability to pay taxes. However, not all property taxes can be discharged in bankruptcy, and tax debts that are tied to fraud or recent returns may not be eligible for repayment under a bankruptcy plan. It's essential to consult with a local bankruptcy attorney to understand the specific impact bankruptcy could have on your tax situation and explore the best path forward.

When it comes to managing IRS tax liabilities, there are several options available that can help alleviate your financial burden and potentially improve your credit score over time. One of the first options to consider is consulting with a CPA, tax attorney, or even the

Options and Strategies for Resolving Credit Entries

IRS directly to determine if you qualify for an "**Offer in Compromise**" (OIC). This program allows taxpayers to negotiate a reduction in their outstanding tax liabilities, making it possible to settle for less than the full amount owed. There are specific qualifications and restrictions for this option, such as demonstrating an inability to pay the full debt, but it can be a useful tool for those facing overwhelming tax debts. While legal representation is not required to pursue an OIC, seeking professional advice can help ensure you meet the necessary criteria and maximize your chances of approval. For more information on the process, it's recommended to contact your local IRS office.

Another potential option for dealing with IRS tax liabilities is filing for bankruptcy. In certain cases, you may be able to include your tax debt in a Chapter 13 bankruptcy repayment plan, allowing you to pay off the debt over 3 to 5 years, depending on your financial situation. It's important to note that not all types of tax debt are dischargeable in bankruptcy, so it's crucial to consult with a bankruptcy attorney to determine if this is a viable option for you.

Additionally, IRS taxes have a 10-year statute of limitations, meaning they can expire if the IRS does not take action to renew the debt after 10 years from the date the tax was assessed. If the IRS does not renew the debt within that time frame, the liability is erased, offering taxpayers a chance to walk away from their tax debt. However, this expiration period can be interrupted by various actions, such as filing for bankruptcy or making partial payments, so it's essential to understand how this statute of limitations works in your specific case.

By taking advantage of these options, individuals can potentially reduce their IRS tax liabilities, improve their financial standing, and begin rebuilding their credit score. As unpaid taxes can significantly damage your credit, resolving this debt through any of these methods could have a positive long-term effect on your creditworthiness.

It's important to take legitimate steps when managing your credit report to promote long-term financial stability and avoid potential penalties or the reappearance of negative information after a fraudulent removal by a credit repair agent.

Medical Debt

Medical debt remains one of the most common types of collections found on credit reports, and it can significantly impact a person's credit score. In some cases, even a small medical bill—less than $100—can cause a drop of 50 to 80 points, depending on the person's credit profile. What makes medical debt especially frustrating is that many people don't know they have outstanding balances until they check their credit report or apply for a loan.

Historically, protections existed to give consumers time to resolve these issues before their credit is harmed. Under earlier policies, credit bureaus provided a 180-day grace period before reporting unpaid medical debt, and debts under $500 were excluded entirely. These rules were designed to prevent billing errors and slow insurance processing from damaging someone's financial record. For a time, even medical collections that were paid or being resolved were removed from credit reports.

However, in July 2025, those protections were rolled back. The Consumer Financial Protection Bureau's rule banning medical debt from credit reports was overturned by a federal court. As a result, medical debt of any amount may now appear on credit reports once again, and lenders can legally use it when making credit decisions. This reversal could affect millions of Americans, many of whom were already struggling to manage rising healthcare costs and lapses in insurance coverage.

For borrowers, this means being proactive is more important than ever. Understanding your insurance plan, requesting itemized bills, and following up on billing errors quickly are key to protecting your

Options and Strategies for Resolving Credit Entries

credit. If you do receive a large bill, speak with the hospital's billing department immediately. Many hospitals offer interest-free payment plans, financial assistance programs, or sliding scale fees based on income. Some even have benevolence or charity departments that may forgive part or all of the balance if you qualify. If a medical debt is already on your credit report, you have options. First, verify the debt and dispute any errors. If the balance is accurate, try negotiating directly with the provider or collection agency. Ask for a reduced lump-sum payment in exchange for removing the item from your credit report. Always get any agreement in writing before making a payment. If you have already paid the debt, but it's still showing as unpaid, you can file a dispute with the credit bureaus using your payment documentation as proof.

Ernestine's Story: When the Rules Change Midway

Ernestine is a single mother of two living in Texas. In 2023, she was treated at the ER for a dehydration episode and ended up with a $700 medical bill. Without employer-sponsored insurance, she couldn't pay the balance in full, and it was sent to collections. Fortunately, under the Biden-era protections, that debt didn't appear on her credit report. Her credit score remained intact, and she was even approved for a small car loan in 2024. She used her tax refund to pay down most of the balance and was on a payment plan for the rest. As part of her due diligence, she requested an itemized bill from the hospital. While reviewing it, she noticed she had been charged twice for the same medication. She contacted the benevolence department at the hospital, which agreed to forgive part of her debt. **This brought the amount down to $400.** The Credit bureaus collectively decided April 11, 2023 not to report in Medical debt on credit reports that were under $500.00. Finally, she emailed the credit bureaus to ensure her file was properly updated. That small victory gave her even more motivation to finish paying the bill. But when the new law passed in 2025, everything changed. The remaining debt—now less than $400—reappeared on her credit report due to the reversal of the medical debt reporting rule. Her score dropped by nearly 30 points. When she tried to refinance her auto loan, she was denied.

Rather than give up, Ernestine took action. She pulled her credit reports and disputed the amount that had already been paid. She gathered billing documents and reached out to a local nonprofit for help negotiating the remaining balance. She also contacted the benevolence department at the hospital, which agreed to forgive part of her debt. Finally, she called the credit bureaus to ensure her file was properly updated. It took persistence, but she protected her financial future by staying informed and taking initiative.

What You Can Do

Ernestine's story is a powerful reminder that credit policies can shift, but your knowledge and action make the difference. Here are key strategies to help you stay ahead:

- Always request itemized medical bills and dispute any errors early, before your credit is harmed.
- Communicate with healthcare providers about payment plans or charity care options.
- Use a Health Savings Account (HSA) if available, to reduce out-of-pocket costs.
- Check your credit reports regularly for errors or medical debts that reappear.
- Keep records of all payments, disputes, and agreements in case of future reporting errors.

The financial burden of medical debt is real, but with knowledge, persistence, and a willingness to advocate for yourself, you can protect your credit and move toward financial peace—even when the rules change.

This chart outlines the typical timeframes, but keep in mind that individual situations may differ depending on state laws, the type of debt, and any special actions, such as filing for bankruptcy.

Options and Strategies for Resolving Credit Entries

TYPE OF DEBT	TIME ON CREDIT REPORT
Bankruptcy (Chapter 7)	10 years
Bankrupcy (Chapter 13)	7 years
Late Payments	7 years from the date of the missed payment
Foreclosures	7 years
Tax Liens	7 years (can be renewed for an additional 7 years if not paid)
Collection Accounts	7 years from the date of the last payment or activity
Charged-Off Accounts	7 years from the date of the charge-off
Judgments	7 years (can be renewed in some states)
Repossessions	7 years
Students Loans in Default	7 years (can be rehabiliated or consolidated to remove default status)
Inquiries (Hard)	2 years

The length of time a creditor has to file a lawsuit on a debt is governed by the statute of limitations. The **statute of limitations** refers to the period within which a creditor can file a lawsuit to collect a debt. Once this period has passed, the creditor is legally barred from taking you to court for repayment, though they can still attempt to collect the debt through other means (like phone calls or letters). The statute of limitations varies by debt type and state, ranging generally from **3 to 10 years**.

The following is a breakdown of common debt types and the typical statute of limitations:

DEBT TYPE	TYPICAL STATUE OF LIMITATIONS
Written Contracts (e.g. credit card debt, personal loans)	4-6 years (most states)
Oral Contracts (e.g., verbal agreements)	3-6 years
Promissory Notes (e.g., car loans student loans)	Usually 6 years, varies by state
Open-ended Accounts (e.g., credit cards)	3-6 years

Once the statute of limitations has expired, the creditor can no longer file a lawsuit to collect the debt. However, they may still attempt to collect the debt through other means, but they cannot take legal action. Keep in mind that depending on your state, the statute of limitations can be restarted or tolled if you make a payment, or acknowledge the debt in writing. It's also important to consult with a local attorney to understand the specific laws in your state.

PHASE TWO Q&A AND ACTIONS STEPS

Q&A	QUESTIONS	ANSWER
1	What is the purpose of Phase Two in the credit repair process	Phase Two focuses on handling negative entries that were verified as accurate by creditors. It teaches individuals how to challenge fraudulent entries, negotiate debt settlements, and explore options for bankruptcies, foreclosures students loans and other financial matters.
2	How can 15 U.S. Code § 1692g help in removing collections from your credit report?	This law requires debt collectors to provide validation of the debt if requested within 30 days. If they fail to validate the debt, they must cease collection activities and remove the entry from your credit report. If a collection account is inaccurate or violates debt collection laws, it can also be disputed and potentially deleted.
3	What are the key steps to disputing an inaccurate or fraudulent entry on your credit report?	First, obtain a copy of your credit report and identify incorrect entries. Then, send a dispute letter to the credit bureaus and a debt validation letter to the creditor. If the creditor cannot provide documentation proving the debt's legitimacy, the entry must be removed.
4	Why is it important to get a settlement agreement in writing before paying off debt?	A written agreement ensures that the creditor honors their promise to update or delete the account from your credit report. Without this documentation, the creditor may still report the account as a settled or paid collection, which can continue to affect your credit score.
5	What protections does the Fair Credit Billing Act (FCBA) provide for consumers dealing with fraudulent charges?	The FCBA limits consumer liability for unauthorized charges to $50 and requires creditors to investigate billing disputes. If a fraudulent charge is reported, the creditor must respond within 30 days and resolve the issue within two billing cycles.

Phase Two Q&A and Actions Steps

ACTION STEPS	DESCRIPTION
Step 1: Identify Verified Negative Entries	Review your credit reports and highlight accounts that have been verified as accurate but may still be challenged due to errors, lack of documentation, or fraud.
Step 2: Dispute Collections Using 15 U.S. Code § 1692g	If a collection is questionable, send a debt validation request within 30 days. the collector fails to validate, dispute the entry with the credit bureaus to request its removal.
Step 3: Handle Debt Settlement Strategically	Before making a payment, negotiate with creditors for a pay-for-delete agreement and obtain confirmation in writing before proceeding. This ensures the account is removed from your credit report.
Step 4: Address Bankruptcies, Foreclosures, and Student Loans	Understand legal timeframes for these entries and dispute any inaccuracies. If eligible, use rehabilitation or consolidation programs for student loans to improve credit standing.
Step 5: Protect Against Future Fraud	Freeze your LexisNexis report, monitor your credit regularly, and file disputes immediately if fraudulent entries appear. If needed, consult with a consumer rights attorney.

NOTES

THE TRUTH ABOUT CREDIT

Phase Three

In This Section, You'll Learn How To:

S̲trengthen Y̲our C̲redit

B̲uild and P̲rotect Y̲our C̲redit

- View and Manage Your Credit Scores
- Create and Acquire New Credit

STEP #1: Your Credit Score

Credit scores play a pivotal role in determining an individual's creditworthiness, and various scoring systems exist to assess the likelihood that a person will repay borrowed money. One of the most widely known scoring systems is the **FICO score**, which is used by many lenders to make decisions on whether to extend credit. The Advantage Score, a newer competitor to FICO, is used by some lenders, and several other scoring models also evaluate creditworthiness. Each system has its own way of interpreting financial behaviors, but the general principles of evaluating credit risk remain largely the same: payment history, amounts owed, and credit history length are all crucial components.

FICO SCORE SYSTEM

The **FICO score** is a three-digit number that ranges from **300 to 850**, with **300 being considered poor** and **850 being considered excellent**. This score is calculated using a statistical model that takes real-world data and identifies patterns related to creditworthiness. The FICO score reflects five key categories, each contributing a different weight to the final score:

CATEGORY	PERCENTAGE OF SCORE	DESCRIPTION
Payment History	35%	The most important factor. It tracks whether you have paid your bills on time.
Amount Owed	30%	The total amount of debt you owe, including credit card balances and loans.
Length of Credit History	15%	The duration of your credit history, including how long your accounts have been open.
New Credit	10%	How many new accounts you have opened recently or inquiries made on your credit.
Credit Mix	10%	The variety of credit types you have (credit cards, mortgages, loans, etc.).

When repairing your credit, understanding the categories and their associated percentages can help you prioritize the right actions to boost your score. For example, if you have a debt that has been on your credit report for 10 years, is paid in full, and has never been late, it is positively impacting your score in several key areas: **payment history (35%)**, **amount owed (30%)**, and **length of credit history (15%)**. This means the account is contributing to **80%** of your FICO score. However, if you decide to close this account because you no longer use it, you may see a drop in your credit score. This happens because by closing the account, you're removing the positive impact it had on those crucial areas of your score. In essence, that account was benefiting **80%** of your FICO score, and its closure can cause a noticeable decline in your credit score.

Bringing your credit card balance below the 30% utilization threshold can substantially elevate your credit score. Additionally, I have found that negative entries older than two years, provided they haven't seen any further activity, have a much smaller impact on your score compared to recent delinquencies. Older negative entries

STEP #1: Your Credit Score

lose their weight over time, while new delinquencies can cause a more significant and immediate decline in your credit score.

FICO scores can range from **300 to 850,** and the score determines the interest rates and terms you may be offered when applying for credit. A higher score generally results in better terms, such as lower interest rates. Here's how FICO scores are typically broken down:

FICO SCORE	Credit Rating
300-579	Poor
580-669	Fair
670-739	Good
740-799	Very Good
800 +	Excellent

A **score of 740 or higher** typically qualifies you for the best available interest rates, while a **score below 600** may result in higher rates or difficulty in obtaining credit.

FICO has created several different credit scoring models to fit the needs of different industries and types of loans. Whether it's a mortgage, auto loan, credit card, or someone with little credit history, each model is designed to assess specific risks more accurately. Since different lenders care about different things when evaluating a borrower's creditworthiness, having various FICO scoring systems helps them make better, more informed decisions. These specialized models make sure that credit scores match the type of loan or credit you're applying for, ultimately benefiting both consumers and lenders.

FICO SCORING MODEL	PRIMARY USE	KEY FEATURES
FICO 2, 4, 5	Mortgage Lending	Older versions, more conservative, used by FHA, VA, and conventional loans.
FICO Auto Score	Auto Lending	Focuses on auto loan payment history and car-related behaviors.
FICO Bankcard Score	Credit Card Lending	Focuses on credit card use, balances, and payment history.
FICO SCORE XD	Consumers with Limited Credit History	Uses alternative data sources like utility and rent payments.
FICO Resilience Index	Predicts Financial Hardship Risk	Assesses likelihood of default during economic stress.

STEP #1: Your Credit Score

FICO SCORING MODEL	SCORE RANGE	KEY FEATURES & DIFFERENCES
FICO 8	300 - 850	• The most widely used scoring model. • Emphasizes payment history, amount owed, and length of credit history. • Credit utilization is particularly important; high utilization can have a more significant negative impact. • Tends to be more lenient on isolated missed payments and less focused on medical debt.
FICO 9	300 - 850	• Incorporates medical debt and alternative data (like rental payments). • Medical debt is given less weight than other types of debt, and paid medical collections are ignored. • Does not penalize consumers as harshly for small collections (eg, balances under $100). • Used less frequently than FICO 8 but gaining traction.
FICO 10/10T	300 - 850	• Introduced in 2020, FICO 10 and the updated FICO 10T models place greater emphasis on trends in credit usage, such as credit utilization over time and balance growth. • Increased weight on debt-to-income ratio and credit utilization patterns. • Consumers with high utilization over a period of time will see a significant impact on their scores. • Lenders may use this model for more detailed risk analysis but it's still less common than FICO 8.

Advantage Score System

The **Advantage Score** is a newer credit scoring system *developed by the major credit bureaus to compete with FICO*. Unlike FICO, which uses a specific number range (300 to 850), the Advantage Score uses a **letter grading** system. The score is based on similar factors as the FICO score, such as payment history, amounts owed, and the length of credit history. However, its unique approach eliminates the need for paying a third party (FICO) by offering a proprietary solution.

The Advantage Score assigns a **letter grade** to indicate a consumer's creditworthiness. Here's a breakdown of the letter grade scale:

SCORE RANGE	LETTER GRADE
901-990	A
801-900	B
701-800	C
601-700	D

- **A (901-990)**: Excellent credit, low risk of defaulting on debt.
- **B (801-900)**: Very good credit, favorable terms for loans and credit.
- **C (701-800)**: Good credit, generally acceptable for most lenders.
- **D (601-700)**: Fair credit may face higher interest rates.

The Advantage Score system is still relatively new and has not yet replaced FICO as the dominant credit scoring model. Many businesses are familiar and comfortable with FICO, making the switch to a new system unlikely for the foreseeable future. However, the Advantage Score could potentially become a more widely adopted system in the coming years as more companies seek to avoid paying FICO for using their model.

Other Credit Scoring Systems
In addition to FICO and Advantage Score, there are other credit scoring systems used by lenders and financial institutions. These include:

1. **VantageScore**: This scoring model, developed by the three major credit bureaus (Equifax, Experian, and TransUnion), is similar to FICO in terms of factors like payment history,

STEP #1: Your Credit Score

credit usage, and credit age. VantageScore ranges from **300 to 850** and is divided into categories similar to FICO:

VANTAGE SCORE RANGE	CREDIT RATING
300-499	Poor
500-600	Fair
601-660	Good
661-780	Very Good
781-850	Excellent

2. **Experian's PLUS Score**: This is another alternative credit score provided by Experian, which is similar to FICO and VantageScore, but it uses a different method of calculation. The PLUS score also ranges from **330 to 830**, and it considers factors such as your total debt, payment history, and usage of credit.

3. **TransUnion's Credit Vision Score**: This model uses a range of **300 to 850** and places more emphasis on recent credit activity and trends rather than just the static credit report. It helps lenders understand how a person manages credit at a given time.

While *FICO remains the most widely used credit scoring system*, with its detailed breakdown of how various factors influence your score, other systems like Advantage Score, VantageScore, and others have begun to challenge its dominance. Whether you're evaluating your own creditworthiness, or a lender is deciding whether to extend you credit, it's important to understand the system in play and how your financial behavior impacts your score.

To summarize, here's how the scores from various models compare:

SCORE RANGE	FICO	VANTAGE SCORE	ADVANTAGE SCORE
Excellent	800-850	781-850	A (901-990)
Very Good	740-799	661-780	B (801-900)
Good	670-739	601-660	C (701-800)
Fair	580-669	500-600	D (601-700)
Poor	300-579	300-499	–

Raising your Credit Score

Let's talk about why it's so important to raise your credit score and how it can be lowered. As we mentioned earlier, it's essential to check your credit reports from all bureaus, since creditors may have memberships with one bureau but not the others. This means that the information you see could vary. Just as important is checking your **FICO score** with each bureau, because each one can give you a different score. Creditors usually take the **middle score** from the three, so it's vital to monitor all of them to get an accurate understanding of where you stand.

The big question is: "How can I raise my credit score so I can buy a TV without having to rent one and pay five times its value?" Or "How can I avoid being stuck at a 'tote-the-note' car dealership and instead shop at a place where I can get a car with fewer miles, a lower interest rate, and much lower monthly payments?" Another area where people are often taken advantage of is when they purchase a home with an adjustable-rate mortgage (ARM) instead of a fixed-rate mortgage. The allure of a lower monthly payment can be tempting, but many aren't informed that if the loan isn't refinanced

STEP #1: Your Credit Score

within a certain period, their payments could rise, sometimes dramatically, every six months. I've seen mortgages jump from $1,000 to $1,600 in just a year. The good news is, there are several strategies you can consider to improve your credit:

1. Double-Check Every Detail: It's crucial to double-check that all the information on your credit report is accurate, no matter how minor it may seem. If you've paid off a debt, make sure it's listed as "PAID" and not showing as an outstanding balance simply because the creditor didn't update it. If an account shows as closed later than it actually was, dispute that as well. You have the right to request that the account be **updated** or even **deleted** entirely. By taking these simple steps can help ensure that your credit is accurate and give your score the boost it deserves.

2. Investigate Late Payments Carefully: If you notice any late payments on your credit report, take the time to investigate them thoroughly. Late payments can reduce your score up to **100 points.** If the late payment was caused by a holiday due date, an issue with the creditor's pay-by-phone system, or another valid reason beyond your control, bring this to the attention of a manager. Creditors have the ability to remove these late payments under certain circumstances, especially when there's a clear error or technical issue. Be persistent and assertive. Request that the late payment be **deleted** from your report. This could result in an immediate improvement to your credit score.

I once received a late payment on a major department store credit card because I was very sick and unable to make the payment on time. As a result, the late payment was reported on my credit file. I called the creditor, explained my situation, and pointed out that I had never missed a payment before. As a one-time courtesy, they agreed to remove the late payment from my credit report.

This experience shows that it **is possible to have late payments removed by the creditor**, especially if you have a good payment history and communicate with them promptly. Afterward, I set up automatic payments to help ensure I never missed a due date again

3. Dispute Negative Information Regularly: If you have derogatory information on your credit report, don't hesitate to dispute it, and keep disputing it until the creditor addresses the issue. Under the Fair Credit Reporting Act (FCRA), credit bureaus are required to investigate any dispute within **30 days**, and if they cannot verify the accuracy of the negative entry, it must be removed from your report. Creditors and collection agencies may get tired of repeatedly responding to disputes, especially if the information is outdated or inaccurate. If a creditor fails to respond within the required time frame, the entry will be deleted, and your credit score could improve. Keep in mind that you should have proper documentation to support your disputes, as this will strengthen your case. Repeated disputes, especially when errors are involved, can help ensure that only accurate, up-to-date information remains on your credit report, leading to an improved credit score.

4. A Discharged Bankruptcy Can Improve Your Credit Score: When a bankruptcy is discharged and properly updated with the credit bureaus, it can lead to an increase in your credit score. While a bankruptcy will initially cause a significant drop in your score, once it's discharged and reflected correctly on your credit report, the impact of the bankruptcy lessens over time. In some cases, I've personally seen credit scores increase by as much as **50-100 points** immediately after the discharge is recorded. This happens because the credit bureaus update the status of the bankruptcy, indicating that the debtor has completed the process and is no longer actively in debt. Additionally, once the bankruptcy is officially discharged, you can begin rebuilding your credit by focusing on making on-time payments and managing your finances responsibly. It's essential to ensure the discharge is properly updated to reflect that you are no longer liable for the debts included in the bankruptcy, as this can significantly improve your creditworthiness moving forward.

STEP #1: Your Credit Score

5. Negotiate Deletion of Collection Entries: Many collection agencies are willing to remove a negative entry from your credit report if you pay the debt in full. This practice, known as "pay for delete," can significantly improve your credit score by removing the derogatory mark associated with the debt. When negotiating with a collection agency, ask them directly: "Do you delete the entry upon full payment?" If they agree, insist on getting the arrangement in writing before you make any payment. This written agreement should clearly state that the collection entry will be deleted from your credit report once the specified amount is paid. It's crucial not to send any funds until you have the written confirmation, as this ensures you're protected and can hold the agency accountable. Keep in mind that not all creditors or collection agencies will agree to delete the entry, but it's worth attempting. If successful, this can significantly boost your credit score by removing a major negative item from your credit history.

6. Keep Your Credit Card Balances Under 30% of Your Limit: One of the easiest ways to improve your credit score is by making sure your credit card balances stay under 30% of your available credit. For example, if your credit limit is $5,000, try to keep your balance at $1,500 or less. This not only helps keep your utilization low but also shows creditors that you're handling your credit responsibly. The lower your utilization rate, the better it looks on your credit report, and it can have a significant positive impact on your score. It tells lenders that you're not overly reliant on credit, which is a key indicator of financial health. If you happen to max out one of your cards but are offered a higher credit limit (say, $15,000), this could be a great opportunity to transfer the balance over. Doing so will help you stay under the 30% utilization rate, which over time can help boost your credit score. But be cautious. **Don't start spending more** just because you have a higher limit. Stick to the 30% rule, and you'll keep your credit utilization in check, leading to a better credit score. Building good credit takes time and discipline, but with consistency, you'll see the benefits.

7. Disputing Incorrect Credit Balances Online Can Lead to Faster Updates: If you spot an error or an outdated entry on your credit report, disputing it online can be a quick way to get it resolved. In many cases, when you file a dispute online, credit bureaus may update your information within **10 days**, much faster than the standard **30-day window** they typically have to resolve disputes. This faster turnaround means that any corrections, whether it's a mistake in your credit balance or an outdated account, can be reflected in your score more quickly, giving you the chance to see a score improvement sooner.

8. Call Your Creditor to Correct Your Balance Quickly: If you notice an error on your credit report, contacting your creditor directly can sometimes result in a much faster resolution than waiting for the typical 30 to 60-day processing time. By calling the creditor and requesting that they update your balance immediately, you may be able to have the correction made much sooner. Some creditors, especially those with more streamlined systems, can make updates to the credit bureaus in as little as **a few days**, instead of the standard 30 to 60 days.

9. Get Added as an Authorized User to Boost Your Credit: One effective way to improve your credit score, especially if you're just starting to build credit or working to repair it, is by having someone with good credit add you as an authorized user on their credit card. Ideally, the card should have a long history of on-time payments and a low balance, as this will help you benefit from their positive credit activity.

As an authorized user, you don't need to use the card or even be responsible for the payments. Instead, the credit history associated with that account, including **timely payments, low balances,** and **responsible usage**, gets reported on your credit report as if it's your own. This can give your credit score a significant boost, especially if your credit history is limited or includes negative entries. It's also important to note that if the primary cardholder fails to make

STEP #1: Your Credit Score

payments on time, that negative information will also appear on your credit report. Late payments or high balances on the account can harm your credit score just as much as they would for the primary cardholder. So, make sure you're added to an account with someone who has a strong history of timely payments. By choosing wisely, this strategy can be a fast and effective way to improve your credit.

10. Maintain 3 to 5 Lines of Credit for a Healthy Credit Profile: Keeping 3 to 5 lines of credit is often viewed as the sweet spot for a strong credit score. Having too many accounts can seem excessive and may negatively affect your score. For example, you could have three credit cards, each with a balance under 30% of the credit limit, along with a home mortgage and a car loan. This type of credit mix is not only manageable but also beneficial. A good mix of credit types (credit cards, installment loans, etc.) makes up 10% of your FICO score, demonstrating to lenders that you can handle various kinds of debt responsibly. Having a balanced credit portfolio helps showcase financial stability, keeping your score in a healthy range without overextending yourself.

11. Request a Credit Limit Increase to Boost Your Score

Why it works: Requesting a credit limit increase can be an effective way to improve your credit score by lowering your **credit utilization ratio**, which is the percentage of your available credit that you're using. A lower utilization ratio indicates to lenders that you're managing your credit responsibly, which can positively impact your score. For example, if you have a credit card with a $2,000 limit and a current balance of $1,000 (which gives you a 50% utilization rate), requesting a credit limit increase to $4,000 will reduce your utilization to 25%, assuming you don't increase your spending. This drop in utilization could lead to an improvement in your score. It's crucial to approach this strategy with caution. If you're granted a higher limit, resist the temptation to rack up more debt. Only request a credit limit increase if you're confident that you won't overspend.

Using more available credit can backfire, so stick to a disciplined approach.

Keep in mind that **credit utilization accounts for about 30%** of your FICO score, making it one of the most significant factors. A lower utilization ratio not only boosts your score but also signals to lenders that you're in control of your finances. This is a simple, yet powerful way to increase your score over time without taking on more debt.

12. Use a Secured Loan and Secured Credit Card to Build or Rebuild Your Credit

Why it works: If you're new to credit or working to rebuild a low score, using a credit-building loan combined with a credit card can be a powerful strategy to improve your credit. These tools are designed to help establish or repair your credit by showing that you're capable of managing debt responsibly. Both the credit-building loan and the credit card report your timely payments to the credit bureaus, which helps boost your credit score over time.

A **Secured loan** works by having you borrow a small amount of money, which is held in a savings account or CD until you've repaid it. As you make regular payments, the financial institution reports your activity to the credit bureaus, showing that you're handling the loan responsibly. Making consistent, on-time payments is essential since your payment history makes up 35% of your FICO score. So the more positive payment history you build, the better your score will become.

Using a credit building credit card works similarly. If you have a secured credit card or a starter card, you'll need to make sure you're using it responsibly. Keeping your balance *under 30%* of the card's limit and paying it off on time every month shows the credit bureaus that you are able to manage credit without overspending. Your credit utilization (how much of your available credit you're using) makes up 30% of your FICO score, so keeping your utilization low can have a significant impact on your score.

For example, let's say you open a secured credit card with a $500 limit and make small purchases every month that you can pay off in full. If you also take out a credit-building loan for $500 and make the required monthly payments, both of these actions will be reported to the credit bureaus. Over time, the combination of responsible credit card use and timely loan payments will gradually improve your credit score.

The positive effects are **cumulative**. As you make on-time payments on both your credit card and loan, your credit score will increase, especially as your credit utilization ratio improves and your payment history builds. For someone with little or no credit history, this strategy can lead to a noticeable improvement in your score within just a few months. It's important to be consistent, as both tools work best when you show that you can handle credit in a responsible way.

In addition, having both a credit card and a loan on your report helps show a **healthy mix of credit types**, which is another factor that can positively impact your score. This can open doors to better credit offers, such as lower interest rates or higher credit limits, down the road.

13. Keep Old Accounts Open to Protect Your Credit Score

Why it works: The length of your credit history makes up 15% of your FICO score, so the longer your credit history, the better it is for your score. When you close old accounts, you shorten your credit history, which can lead to a lower score. Even if you don't use the card, it's usually better to leave it open with a zero balance.

14. Use Rent and Utility Payments to Build Your Credit

Why it works: Many credit bureaus now allow you to report your rent, utility, and phone payments, helping to boost your credit score. For example, services like **Experian Boost** let you link your utility accounts (such as water, electricity, and even your phone bill) directly to your credit file. This means your on-time payments for these regular bills can contribute to your credit history, which is a great way to build or improve your credit score, especially if you have little or no traditional credit history.

By adding these types of payments to your credit report, you can demonstrate your ability to manage financial obligations. This is particularly beneficial for people who might not have credit cards or loans but consistently pay rent or utilities on time. Since payment history makes up 35% of your FICO score, every positive payment can have a real impact on your score.

This service is especially helpful for those who may be new to credit or are trying to rebuild their score after financial difficulties. Plus, it's an easy way to get credit for things you're already paying for, making it a win-win! Just be sure to keep those payments consistent, as missed or late payments will negatively affect your score.

15. Consolidate Your Debt

Why it works: If you're juggling multiple high-interest debts, consolidating them into one loan with a lower interest rate can help lighten your financial load and improve your credit score. By simplifying your payments into a single monthly bill, it's easier to stay on track and avoid missing payments, which is key to boosting your score.

For example, let's say you have credit cards with 20% interest rates and a personal loan with a high rate as well. If you qualify for a debt consolidation loan at a lower interest rate, you could pay off all those balances and focus on one loan with a more manageable rate. Not only will this reduce the overall interest you're paying, but it will also lower your credit utilization (the amount of credit you're using compared to your available credit), which makes up 30% of your FICO score.

It's important to note that consolidation only helps if you don't start racking up more debt after paying everything off. If you keep your credit card balances low and focus on paying off your consolidation loan, you should see improvements in your score over time. It's all about reducing your debt and showing that you can manage your finances responsibly.

16. Limit Hard Inquiries

Why it works: Each time you apply for credit, a "hard inquiry" is added to your credit report, which can cause a temporary dip in your score. This happens because lenders want to assess your creditworthiness before offering you a loan or credit card. However, too many hard inquiries in a short time frame can raise a red flag to lenders, signaling that you might be desperate for credit or taking on more debt than you can manage. This can make you appear as a higher-risk borrower, which can hurt your chances of approval.

For example, constantly applying for store credit cards to get discounts on in-store purchases might seem like a good idea in the moment, but each application can negatively impact your score. These inquiries can pile up quickly, and lenders may view your behavior as a sign that you're overextending yourself financially.

Instead of applying for multiple credit cards or loans, try to limit your hard inquiries to only when absolutely necessary. If you don't need extra credit right away, it's better to wait until you're in a strong financial position before applying for new credit. Taking a more cautious approach can help maintain your score

17. Pay Bills on Time (Every Time)

Why it works: Payment history makes up 35% of your FICO score, so paying bills on time is crucial. Consistently making timely payments shows creditors you're reliable, which boosts your score. One late payment can harm your credit, so setting up automatic payments or reminders can help keep you on track. Over time, staying punctual with your bills can significantly improve your score and make you more appealing to lenders.

A late payment can lower your credit score by as much as 90 to 100 points depending on factors like how late the payment is and your overall credit history. For example:

- **30 days late**: A first-time 30-day late payment could lower your score by 60-110 points, especially if you have a high credit score.
- **60-90 days late**: A payment 60-90 days late can cause a bigger drop, potentially 100+ points.
- **120 days late or more**: The longer the delay, the more it can hurt your score, especially if it escalates to collections.

Staying on top of due dates and paying bills on time can prevent this damage and help maintain a positive credit score.

18. Co-Signers and Joint Accounts

When you co-sign a loan or open a joint account with someone, you are taking on full responsibility for that debt, just as if you had borrowed the money yourself. Many people don't realize that if the other person misses a payment, it will negatively impact your credit too. Co-signing can help someone qualify for credit they couldn't get on their own, but it also puts your own financial future at risk.

Similarly, joint accounts, such as shared credit cards or loans, report to both individuals' credit reports. Good payment history can help both parties' scores but missed payments or high balances will hurt both equally. Before co-signing or opening a joint account, make sure you trust the other person's financial habits, and be prepared for the responsibility that comes with sharing credit.

Lowering the Credit Score

1. Re-aging of debt occurs when a creditor or debt collector updates the status of a debt to make it appear newer than it is, often resetting the "clock" on negative information. This can make it look like an old

STEP #1: Your Credit Score

debt is still active, which can cause your credit score to drop significantly. The FICO scoring model places a high value on the recency of negative marks, so re-aging can extend the time a debt impacts your credit. For example, if a debt was originally marked as late or charged-off, re-aging it could make it seem like the issue is more recent, potentially extending the negative impact for years.

Re-aging of debt is illegal if done without your consent or in a way that manipulates your credit unfairly. The **Fair Credit Reporting Act (FCRA)** requires that all information reported to credit bureaus must be accurate, including the dates of delinquencies. If a creditor re-ages a debt without proper documentation or justification, it can violate consumer protection laws like the **Fair Debt Collection Practices Act (FDCPA)**. If you suspect re-aging, check your credit report, dispute any inaccuracies with the credit bureaus, and contact the creditor for clarification.

2. High Credit Balances

How it works: Credit utilization, the ratio of your credit card balance to your credit limit, makes up 30% of your FICO score. Keeping high balances can damage your score because it signals to lenders that you're over-relying on credit. For example, if you have a $5,000 credit limit and consistently carry a balance close to the max, it can hurt your credit score by up to 100 points. On the flip side, keeping your credit utilization under 30% (or ideally around 25% to 35%) can help improve your score.

Example: Imagine you have a $5,000 limit but are carrying a balance of $4,500. That's 90% of your credit limit, which can negatively impact your score. If you reduce that balance to $1,500 (30%), your score could improve significantly.

3. Divorce can have an unexpected impact on your credit, especially if you and your spouse shared joint credit accounts. Even if the divorce decree assigns responsibility for certain debts to one spouse, you may still be held accountable for those debts if they're not paid.

For example, if your spouse was supposed to take over a joint credit card but failed to make payments, the late payments will show up on your credit report, regardless of the divorce agreement.

These missed payments can significantly harm your credit score, as payment history makes up 35% of your FICO score. This means that late or missed payments can drag down your score. To protect your credit during and after a divorce, it's crucial to remove your name from any joint accounts and make sure all debts are properly divided and paid. If you notice any inaccuracies on your credit report, dispute them right away.

> **Proverbs 22:26–27 (NIV):**
>
> *"Do not be one who shakes hands in pledge or puts up security for debts; if you lack the means to pay, your very bed will be snatched from under you."*

This verse warns against cosigning or guaranteeing someone else's debt. Even with good intentions, you are taking a serious risk: if the other person fails to pay, you become fully responsible, and it could cost you everything you have. God's Word teaches us to be wise and cautious in financial decisions, protecting ourselves and our families from unnecessary hardship.

4. Late Payments, Charge-Offs, Liens, Bankruptcy, Foreclosures, and Collections

How it works: These are major red flags for lenders. Payment history accounts for 35% of your FICO score, meaning one missed payment can cause significant damage. Charge-offs, liens, and bankruptcies can impact your score for up to 7 years. A single late payment could lower your score by up to 100 points, depending on how long your credit history is and how severe the late payment is.

Example: If you miss a payment on your car loan, the lender may report it to the credit bureaus, which can cause an immediate drop in your score. For instance, if you've been paying on time for years, a 30-day late payment could result in a 75-point drop. If the missed payment turns into a charge-off, your score could drop by 100 points or more.

5. Credit Counseling and Late Payments by a Credit Counseling Agency

How it works: While credit counseling is supposed to help you get back on track, if the agency doesn't manage your payments correctly or delays them, it can harm your score. This typically happens when the agency pays bills late or doesn't fully resolve the debt in a timely manner. A **debt management plan (DMP)** may reduce your balances over time, but it can also show up on your credit report, which may impact your credit score negatively in the short term.

Example: If you enroll in a debt management program and the agency makes a late payment, your score could be hit with a 50–100 point drop. The longer you take to pay off your debts, the longer it stays on your credit report, potentially hurting your score for years.

6. Co-signing for someone can seem like a kind and helpful gesture, but it comes with significant risks. If the person you co-sign for fails to make payments, you become fully responsible for the debt. The creditor can take legal action against you, including filing a lawsuit to recover the amount owed.

7. Applying for Too Many New Accounts

How it works: Each time you apply for a credit card, loan, or even an apartment rental, it can trigger a hard inquiry on your credit report. Hard inquiries reduce your score by 5 to 10 points each time, and too many inquiries in a short period can raise a red flag to lenders. They may see you as someone who is desperate for credit, which can make them hesitant to approve your application.

Example: Imagine you've recently applied for three new credit cards within a short period to increase your available credit. While a single hard inquiry might only lower your score by 5 to 10 points, having multiple inquiries in a short span (specially if you're new to credit or have few accounts) can have a compounding effect. In total, your score could drop by 20 to 30 points or more, depending on your overall credit profile. Inquiries typically stay on your credit report for two years, but only affect your FICO score for the first 12 months. It's also important to note that applying for multiple cards at once may signal risk to lenders, which can further impact your creditworthiness.

8. High-risk lenders are typically companies that offer loans with unfavorable terms, targeting borrowers with poor credit or limited financial options. Examples of these lenders include payday loan providers, title loan lenders, and subprime lenders. Payday loans, for instance, come with short repayment terms and extremely high interest rates, leading to a cycle of debt. Title loans use your vehicle as collateral, often offering high-interest rates and short repayment windows. Subprime lenders cater to individuals with poor credit, but the loans they offer usually come with much higher fees than traditional bank loans, making them more expensive in the long run.

When you have high-risk loans or "lenders of last resort" listed on your credit report, it can significantly damage your overall financial profile and outlook. This is because such loans signal to future creditors that you may be a higher-risk borrower. For example, payday loans or rent-to-own stores might seem like quick fixes, but they can lead to missed payments and added debt, ultimately affecting your credit. Instead of resorting to these types of loans, consider alternatives like credit unions or personal loans from reputable lenders. These options often offer better terms and lower interest rates, helping you avoid the long-term financial damage high-risk loans can cause.

Summary: Every financial choice, from carrying high balances on credit cards to co-signing for a friend, can affect your credit score. Actions like re-aging debt, late payments, and borrowing from high-

STEP #1: Your Credit Score

risk lenders can cause significant damage to your score, impacting your ability to secure loans or favorable interest rates in the future. By managing your credit wisely, paying bills on time, and applying for new credit cautiously, you can protect your score from these common pitfalls. Being proactive, intentional and wise about your credit can help you build and maintain a prosperous financial future.

STEP #2: Creating and Acquiring Credit

We will begin creating and acquiring credit to boost our score and reach our financial goals.

Several credit card companies offer cards to individuals with little or no credit history. While these cards may have high fees, often deducted from your balance upfront, they provide an opportunity to start building a positive credit history. Alternatively, secured credit cards require a deposit that becomes your credit limit. It's essential to ensure that the company reports to the credit bureaus when considering this option.

For instance, someone looking to establish credit might apply for a secured credit card with a $500 deposit, which serves as collateral and becomes the credit limit. By using the card for small purchases each month and paying off the balance in full and on time, positive payment history is reported, slowly improving the credit score. After six months, the individual could apply for a secured loan of $1,000, making payments over the next year. Responsible management of credit will continue to improve the score, opening the door to unsecured loans and better credit card terms. Both the secured credit card and loan lay the foundation for solid credit, paving the way for more financial opportunities.

Understanding Credit Card Types: Choosing the Right Card for You

Not all credit cards are created equal.

Depending on your financial goals and credit history, the type of credit card you choose can make a big difference in your financial journey.

Here's a closer look at the different kinds of credit cards available, so you can choose the one that fits your needs and helps you build a strong credit profile.

Secured Cards

Secured credit cards are perfect for people who are new to credit or rebuilding after financial difficulties.

To open a secured card, you must provide a security deposit, usually equal to your credit limit. Your usage is reported to the credit bureaus, helping you build or rebuild your credit responsibly.

Pros:

- Easier to qualify if you have poor or no credit.
- Can transition to an unsecured card with good payment history over time.

Cons:

- Requires an upfront deposit.
- May have higher fees and lower initial limits.

Tip:

Use your secured card just like a regular credit card, keep your balance low and pay it off on time every month to build strong credit history.

STEP #2: Creating and Acquiring Credit

Unsecured Credit Cards

An **unsecured credit card** doesn't require a deposit.

Instead, your approval is based on your creditworthiness... your credit history, income, and other factors. Some unsecured cards are designed specifically for people with fair or limited credit, offering a starting point for credit building without needing upfront money.

Pros:

- No deposit required.
- Can graduate to better cards with higher limits and lower interest over time.

Cons:

- May come with higher interest rates and fees if your credit is limited or damaged.
- Lower starting limits compared to prime credit cards.

Tip:

Look for unsecured cards that report to all three credit bureaus and avoid cards with excessive fees ("fee-harvester cards").

Retail Store Cards

Retail store credit cards are issued by specific stores or brands and can usually only be used at that store (or a family of stores). Some offer discounts, rewards, or special financing for store purchases.

Pros:

- Easier to qualify even with lower credit scores.
- Good for occasional discounts or promotional financing.

Cons:

- High interest rates if balances aren't paid in full.
- Limited use outside the issuing store or brand.

Tip:

Retail cards can help build credit, but only if used sparingly. Don't carry a large balance just to get a small discount at the checkout.

Student Cards

Student credit cards are designed specifically for college students who are beginning to establish credit.

They often have lower credit limits and may come with educational resources to encourage responsible usage.

Pros:

- Easier approval for students with little to no credit history.
- Some offer cash back rewards and lower fees.

Cons:

- Lower spending limits.
- Interest rates can be high if balances are carried.

Tip:

A student card can be a great first step toward building credit, however, it's important to use it responsibly from day one.

Here are two great options to help you start building or rebuilding your credit:

Discover it – Secured Credit Card
Website: https://www.discover.com/credit-cards/secured/
1-800-347-2683

STEP #2: Creating and Acquiring Credit

The Discover it® Secured card offers cashback rewards and no annual fee. It also provides a free FICO® score on your monthly statements.

Citi Secured Mastercard
Website: https://www.citi.com/credit-cards/credit-card-details/citi-secured-mastercard
1-800-950-5114

Citi's secured card is ideal for those looking to build or rebuild credit. It requires a security deposit and offers access to online account management.

Wells Fargo Secured Credit Card
Website: https://www.wellsfargo.com/credit-cards/secured/
1-800-869-3557

When picking a credit card, it is important to consider your goals, whether you are focused on building credit, earning rewards, or both, while also being honest about whether you can pay off the balance each month and if the fees or interest rates are truly worth the benefits. Choosing the right card and using it wisely can help you strengthen your credit score, unlock better financial opportunities, and even put extra rewards back in your pocket. The key is to treat credit as a tool to build your future, not as a trap that creates debt.

Building credit and establishing a relationship with a credit union or bank is definitely a step in the right direction.

When my friend first started building credit, he took out a secured loan with a $500 deposit. He paid off the loan with the same $500, and once the credit union confirmed his on-time payments, he was able to secure a $1,000 unsecured loan. After paying off that loan, he was approved for a $3,000 auto loan. He continued paying off loans, and after three years of building a strong relationship with the credit bureaus, he was able to call and secure a $6,000 loan. The banker sent him the contract by email, and once he signed it, the funds were deposited directly into his credit union account. It was a gradual process, but it worked incredibly well. You'll also notice that many credit unions offer great interest rates on auto loans, and some even offer mortgage loans. Establishing a relationship with a credit union or local bank can be a great strategy for long-term financial success.

Another effective strategy we mentioned earlier is to have someone with good credit add you to one of their accounts as an authorized user. Make sure that they provide the company with your social security number so that the credit is applied to your reports. You don't need to request a card, as they can keep it. By adding you to the account, you'll acquire their credit history from that particular line of credit, whether it's a credit card, loan, or credit line. Keep in mind that if their credit score drops, it can negatively impact your credit as well—especially if you're a co-signer or joint account holder. Make sure the person is financially responsible before agreeing to share credit or take on a joint obligation.

Additionally, credit bureaus have introduced some non-traditional methods for adding credit to personal credit files. These methods are designed to help individuals improve their credit scores, especially those with limited credit histories or those unable to build credit through traditional means.

Some of these unconventional approaches include:

1. Alternative Credit Data is revolutionizing the way credit scores are built, especially for individuals who have little to no traditional credit history. Traditionally, credit reports have focused mainly on credit cards and loan information, but now credit bureaus are expanding their scope to include alternative data, providing a more comprehensive view of an individual's financial habits. This is a game-changer for many, as it offers new opportunities for people to improve their credit scores based on behaviors that reflect responsibility, even without traditional credit accounts.

STEP #2: Creating and Acquiring Credit

Here are some alternative sources that can positively impact your credit score:

- **Rent Payments**: Many credit bureaus now allow rent payments to be included in your credit report. For people who have consistently paid rent on time, this is a great way to show financial reliability, even if you haven't used credit cards or loans.
- **Utility Bills**: Paying utility bills on time—such as electricity, water, internet, and phone—can now be factored into your credit score. This helps individuals with limited credit histories but a strong record of timely payments.
- **Cell Phone Payments**: Timely cell phone bill payments can now be recognized as part of your credit profile by some credit bureaus. This is particularly helpful for those who rely on mobile phones but may not have traditional credit lines.
- **Insurance Premiums**: Insurance companies are increasingly reporting premium payments to credit bureaus. Making regular, on-time insurance payments can enhance your credit report and score over time.

2. Boosting Your Credit Score with Non-Traditional Data

Several credit bureaus are now incorporating *non-traditional data* to help consumers improve their credit scores. These services allow individuals to add alternative payment data, such as utility bills and rent payments, to their credit reports, giving a more comprehensive view of their financial responsibility. These services reflect the industry's growing trend to incorporate non-traditional financial information, making it easier for consumers with limited or no credit history to improve their scores.

   a. **Experian Boost**: This service allows consumers to add utility and cell phone payments to their credit reports. By including on-time payments for these services, users can potentially increase their credit score, offering a more complete picture of their financial reliability. Website: https://www.experian.com/boost

b. **Equifax's Credit Score Boost**: Equifax allows users to add positive data from non-traditional sources like rent payments and utility bills to their credit reports. This feature helps individuals with limited credit histories, or lower scores improve their creditworthiness. Website: https://www.equifax.com

c. **Credit Vision by TransUnion**: TransUnion's Credit Vision leverages alternative data such as rent and utility payments, as well as historical financial information, to provide a broader view of a consumer's credit profile and potentially boost their credit score. Website: https://www.transunion.com

3. Self-Reported Data

Another growing trend in the credit industry has been the use of *self-reported data*. This allows consumers to directly add information, such as positive payment histories for rent, subscriptions, or even gym memberships, to their credit profiles. These types of payments, which might not typically be included in traditional credit reports, can now help improve credit scores. However, credit bureaus generally don't accept direct submissions from individuals. Instead, they rely on businesses and third-party services to provide this data. To incorporate self-reported information, consumers can use specialized services that act as intermediaries, allowing these payments to be considered by the bureaus. Keep in mind that these services typically charge a fee for reporting this data on your behalf

STEP #2: Creating and Acquiring Credit

Here are some options:

a. **Level Credit** - allows you to report your rent payments to major credit bureaus. Website: https://www.levelcredit.com
b. **Rental Kharma** – Reports rent payments to credit bureaus like TransUnion and Equifax. Website: https://www.rentalkharma.com
c. **eCredible** – Lets you report Utility payments and other recurring bills to your credit report. Website: https://ecredable.com
d. **Ultra FICO Score** uses banking history to assess financial behavior and offer a more comprehensive view of creditworthiness. Website: https://www.ultrafico.com
e. **RentReporters** – Report your rent payments to the credit bureaus, helping you build credit with rent history. Website: https://www.rentreporters.com
f. **CreditMyRent** - A service that reports rent payments to all three major credit bureaus (Equifax, TransUnion, and Experian). Website: https://www.creditmyrent.com
g. **RentTrack** - is a service that allows tenants to report their rent payments to the major credit bureaus (Equifax, Experian, and TransUnion). Website: https://www.renttrack.com
h. **ClearNow** – Another service that reports rent payments to credit bureaus, helping renters build credit. Website: https://www.clearnow.com

4. Credit Builder Loans

Some companies offer credit builder loans, which are small loans designed to help individuals build or rebuild their credit. These loans typically have low amounts, and the payments are reported to the credit bureaus, allowing borrowers to gradually improve their credit history. Many credit bureaus accept credit builder loan information, making them a valuable tool for those looking to strengthen their credit profiles over time. All of these services report both positive and negative information to the credit bureaus, meaning that missed payments can hurt your credit score, while on-time payments can help improve it. Most credit builder loans come with some kind of fee, such as an application or administrative fee, or may require you to set aside funds as a deposit, like with Chime. Be sure to review the specific terms and fees for each service before committing.

Below are some companies that provide credit builder loans:

   a. **Self** - Offers a credit builder loan that allows consumers to build credit while saving money in a secured account. Website: https://www.self.inc
   b. **Credit Builder Plus by DCU** - DCU - offers a credit-build loan option where members can borrow a small amount and make regular payments that are reported to the credit bureaus. Website: **https://www.dcu.org**
   c. **Chime Credit Builder** - While Chime's main offering is a secured credit card, their services function similarly to a credit builder loan, helping users build credit through responsible use. Website: https://www.chime.com
   d. **EasyCredit Builder Loan** - Offers credit builder loans to help improve credit scores by reporting payments to the major credit bureaus. Website: https://www.easycreditbuilderloan.com

5. Personal Loan or Credit Line Accounts for Credit Building

Some lenders and services offer **secured credit lines** or **small personal loans** that can be used to help improve a credit score by reporting on-time payments. These types of credit accounts can be particularly beneficial for individuals with limited or no credit history, as they help build a positive credit record. Below are a few companies that provide such options:

STEP #2: Creating and Acquiring Credit

a. Discover it® Secured Credit Card Website: https://www.discover.com
b. Capital One® Secured Mastercard® Website: https://www.capitalone.com
c. OpenSky® Secured Visa® Credit Card Website: https://www.openskycc.com
d. Self Credit Builder Account Website: https://www.self.inc
e. SeedFi Credit Builder Loan Website: https://www.seedfi.com
f. Credit One Bank® Platinum Visa® for Rebuilding Credit Website: https://www.creditonebank.com

6. Alternative Scoring Models

In addition to traditional FICO scores, there are now **alternative credit scoring models** that can take into account non-traditional data points, such as **VantageScore**. VantageScore and other alternative models often place less emphasis on traditional credit accounts and consider factors like payment history on non-traditional accounts, public records, and **social media activity** to evaluate creditworthiness. These models are designed to provide a broader view of an individual's financial behavior, particularly for those with limited or no credit history in traditional credit reporting systems. It's important to note that these alternative methods are still being refined and are not yet widely adopted across all industries.

For example, alternative scoring models might take into account:

a. **Social Media Activity**: Some models may analyze an individual's social media engagement and behavior. Positive interactions on platforms like LinkedIn, or showing professional accomplishments, might be seen as an indicator of stability and responsibility. Additionally, the strength and quality of social connections could provide insights into an individual's character and financial reliability.

b. **Payment History on Non-Traditional Accounts**: Alternative models might incorporate payment data from things like rent, utilities, and even subscriptions to streaming services. Timely payments on these types of accounts can show a consumer's financial responsibility even if they have little or no traditional credit history.
c. **Public Records**: Information from public records, such as eviction records, tax liens, or court judgments, can be used to assess creditworthiness. Some alternative models may use these records more extensively than traditional credit scores. Information from public records—such as eviction filings, tax liens, bankruptcies, or court judgments—can also be used to assess your creditworthiness. While traditional credit scores tend to focus mainly on loan and credit card activity, some alternative credit scoring models place heavier weight on these public records to evaluate your financial behavior. For example, if someone had an eviction filed against them—even if they eventually paid the overdue rent—the filing itself could still appear in public records and negatively impact how lenders view them. Similarly, an unpaid tax lien could signal to lenders that you have had trouble managing significant financial obligations. Even if these events don't appear directly on your traditional credit report, alternative models may still capture and use them to calculate risk.
d. Because public records are legal documents, they often carry a strong influence on your overall financial profile in alternative scoring systems. It's important to periodically check your public record history and resolve any issues, as they can quietly affect your ability to qualify for loans, rentals, or even job opportunities.
e. **Banking Data**: Some models incorporate information about an individual's bank account activity, such as consistent deposits, savings habits, and the frequency of transactions. This can give lenders a deeper view of a person's overall financial health.

STEP #2: Creating and Acquiring Credit

f. **Educational Background**: In some cases, alternative models may even factor in educational achievements or career progress, especially when these indicators suggest a stable and upward trajectory.

7. Credit Builder Apps and Programs

There are several **credit builder apps** and programs designed to help individuals improve their credit scores by providing tools that report to the credit bureaus. These services allow users to build credit through activities like making everyday purchases, setting up automatic payments, and using financial education resources. These apps and programs help individuals improve their credit score by providing easy-to-use tools for everyday financial management and credit-building.

Here are a few companies that offer credit-building apps and programs:

a. **Chime** - provides a **Credit Builder** credit card with no annual fees or interest, allowing users to build credit by making purchases and paying off the balance. Website: https://www.chime.com
b. **Brigit** - offers credit-building tools alongside personal finance management, including automatic savings and access to small cash advances. Website: https://www.hellobrigit.com
c. **Credit Karma's Score Builder** - a free tool that helps users improve their credit by offering personalized suggestions, such as how to optimize credit card usage and set up automatic payments. Website: https://www.creditkarma.com
d. **Self** - provides a **credit builder account** that allows you to build credit while saving money in a secured account. Website: https://www.self.inc

e. **Petal** - offers a **Petal Visa Credit Card**, which helps users build credit through responsible use and reports to the major credit bureaus. Website: https://www.petalcard.com

8. Assume Responsibility of payments

If you're taking over payments on something like a car, boat, or even a computer, it's really important to keep track of all your payments. After you've been making those payments for a while, you can go to the creditor with the original person on the loan and ask to be added to the account. Explain that you've been handling the payments for an extended period, and in some cases, the creditor might agree to add you. This way, they have another person to collect from if the account ever falls behind. It's just a good way to protect yourself and make sure your efforts are recorded, especially if anything goes wrong down the line.

   a. **Car loan**: If you've been paying off the car for someone, you can ask to be added to the loan account to show you're now responsible for it.
   b. **Boat loan**: Same with a boat loan. If you've been covering the payments, the lender might recognize you as a co-borrower.
   c. **Personal loan**: If you're helping a friend or family member pay off a personal loan, talk to the creditor to make sure you're officially added to the account.

These new methods are making a real difference for people who've struggled to build credit. Whether you're dealing with little to no credit history, you're new to the country, or you just prefer to avoid credit cards, these fresh approaches give you a chance to improve your credit score without relying on traditional methods.

What's great is that many of these tools use things you're already paying for, like rent, utilities, or subscriptions, to help boost your score. You don't need a credit card to show you're financially responsible. This shift makes it easier for anyone to build a solid financial foundation and open up opportunities for better loan terms and lower interest rates. What's important is that each small step you take puts you closer to the financial freedom you deserve! Stay focused and know that building your credit is a journey worth taking.

It is my prayer that *The Truth About Credit* will be the key that unlocks a fresh start and leads you toward a brighter financial future.

As **Joshua 1:9** reminds us,

"Be strong and courageous. Do not be afraid; do not be discouraged, for the Lord your God will be with you wherever you go."

There's no one-size-fits-all solution to building credit.

The best strategy is to choose the option that fits your situation, commit to responsible use, and give your credit history time to grow.

Whether it's a secured card, unsecured card, credit builder loan, or authorized user account, the principles stay the same: **pay on time, keep balances low, and stay consistent.**

Good credit isn't built overnight, but every smart step you take moves you closer to financial freedom.

How Paying Off Debt Helps Your Credit

Building strong credit isn't just about using credit wisely, it's also about managing and reducing debt effectively.

The way you choose to pay down your debts can make a huge difference in both your financial health and your credit score. Reducing your debt is one of the most powerful ways to boost your credit. Lower balances improve your credit utilization ratio, a key factor in your credit score, and paying on time consistently strengthens your credit history.

Eliminating debt also reduces your financial stress and opens the door to new opportunities for saving, investing, and building wealth.

Remember:

Every dollar you pay toward your debt today brings you one step closer to freedom tomorrow. No matter which payoff method you choose, the most important thing is to start… and keep going.

You have the power to turn your debt story into a victory story.

There are two popular strategies that have helped millions of people tackle debt successfully: the **Debt Snowball** and the **Debt Avalanche** methods.

The Debt Snowball Method

The **Debt Snowball** method focuses on building momentum by paying off your smallest debts first.

Here's how it works:

- List all your debts from the smallest balance to the largest.
- Make minimum payments on all your debts except the smallest one.
- Put any extra money toward paying off the smallest debt as quickly as possible.
- Once the smallest debt is paid off, move to the next smallest, and so on.

Why It Works:

The debt snowball method is powerful because it creates quick wins.

Each time you eliminate a balance, you feel a boost of motivation and confidence, which helps you stay focused and committed.

Emotionally, it's incredibly satisfying to see debts disappearing one by one.

STEP #2: Creating and Acquiring Credit

The Debt Avalanche Method

The **Debt Avalanche** method focuses on saving the most money by targeting debts with the highest interest rates first.

Here's how it works:

- List all your debts in order from highest to lowest interest rate.
- Make minimum payments on all debts except the one with the highest interest rate.
- Put any extra money toward the debt with the highest interest rate first.
- Once that debt is paid off, move to the next highest interest rate, and so on.

Why It Works:

The debt avalanche method saves you the most money in interest payments over time.

By tackling the most expensive debts first, you reduce the overall cost of your debt more efficiently, even if it takes a little longer to feel the early wins.

Both strategies work.

The best method is the one you will stick with.

- If you need quick motivation and visible progress to stay on track, the **Debt Snowball** might be right for you.
- If you are motivated by saving the most money possible and can stay disciplined, the **Debt Avalanche** could be the smarter financial choice.

Some people even create a hybrid approach: paying off one or two small debts quickly for momentum, then switching to the highest interest debts to maximize savings.

Reducing your debt is one of the most powerful ways to boost your credit score.

Lower balances improve your **credit utilization ratio** — a key factor in your credit score — and paying on time consistently strengthens your credit history.

Eliminating debts also reduces your financial stress and opens up new opportunities for saving, investing, and building wealth.

Remember:

Every dollar you pay toward your debt today brings you one step closer to freedom tomorrow.

No matter which method you choose, the most important thing is to start… and keep going.

You have the power to turn your debt story into a victory story.

Stay diligent and focus on building a better future for yourself and your family. I've seen firsthand how others have benefited from the tools and advice I've shared, and that positive impact continues to spread. Your financial goals are within reach. **Don't give up.** Just as it took time to get to where you are now, give yourself the grace to work your way out. Stay consistent, stay patient, and most importantly, keep moving forward. Great things are ahead!

PHASE THREE - Q&A AND ACTIONS STEPS

Q&A	QUESTIONS	ANSWER
1	What is the difference between a FICO Score and an Advantage Score?	The FICO Score is the most widely used credit scoring model, ranging from 300 to 850, with lenders using different versions for various types of loans. The Advantage Score, developed by major credit bureaus, uses a similar scoring model but categorizes creditworthiness with letter grades (A, B, C. etc.) instead of just numbers.
2	How does credit utilization affect your credit score?	Credit utilization makes up 30% of your FICO score and refers to the amount of credit you are using compared to your total available credit. Keeping utilization below 30% can significantly improve your credit score, while exceeding this threshold can lower it.
3	What are some alternative ways to build credit without a traditional credit card?	Some non-traditional ways to build credit include: reporting rent and utility payments through services like Experian Boost, using credit builder loans, getting added as an authorized user on a credit card, or using secured credit cards that report positive payment history to the credit bureaus.
4	Why is it important to keep old credit accounts open?	Credit history length accounts for 15% of your FICO score. Closing an old account shortens your credit history and can negatively impact your score. Even if you don't use an account often, keeping it open can help maintain strong credit history.
5	How can becoming an authorized user on someone else's credit card help your credit?	If added to a responsible cardholder's account, their positive payment history and low credit utilization can reflect on your report, helping to improve your score. However, if they miss payments or have high balances, it can also negatively affect your credit.

Phase Three - Q&A and Actions Steps

ACTION STEPS	DESCRIPTION
Step 1: Check and Monitor Your Credit Score Regularly	Utilize free services like Credit Karma, Experian, or your bank's FICO score feature to track your credit score and monitor changes over time. Identify areas for improvement, such as reducing balances or disputing incorrect information.
Step 2: Keep Credit Utilization Low	Maintain your credit card balances below 30% of the credit limit to maximize your credit score. If possible, pay off balances in full each month to avoid interest and demonstrate responsible credit management.
Step 3: Build Credit Through Alternative Methods	If you have no or low credit, consider credit builder loans, secured credit cards, rent reporting services, or getting added as an authorized user to establish a solid credit history.
Step 4: Open New Credit Accounts Strategically	If needed, apply for new credit carefully. Avoid opening too many accounts at once, as multiple hard inquiries can lower your score. Focus on low-interest, no-fee options that align with your financial goals.
Step 5: Dispute Errors and Keep Accounts in Good Standing	Regularly review your credit report for errors and dispute inaccuracies with the credit bureaus. Ensure all bills, loans, and credit accounts are paid on time, as payment history accounts for 35% of your FICO score.

NOTES

THE TRUTH ABOUT CREDIT

About the Author

A passionate financial educator and advocate, Jacqueline Willcot has dedicated her life to helping individuals rebuild after financial hardship. Through one-on-one coaching, dynamic seminars, and her published books, she has empowered countless people to break free from the limitations of financial struggle, and take real steps toward lasting stability and independence.

Her mission is simple yet powerful: to replace financial confusion with confidence, and to make financial freedom accessible to anyone willing to learn.

As the oldest of nine children, Jacqueline knew early on that she didn't want to live a life of lack. Determined to create a different future, she immersed herself in financial education and personal growth, equipping herself with the tools to build a life of freedom and purpose. Today, she pours that same passion into helping others do the same. Her work is driven by the belief that with the right knowledge, anyone can rise above their circumstances and create the life they truly deserve.

Sample Letters and Affidavits

DEBT VALIDATION LETTER

[Your Name]

[Your Address]

[City, State, ZIP Code]

[Email Address]

[Phone Number]

[Date]

[Debt Collector's Name]

[Debt Collector's Address]

[City, State, ZIP Code]

RE: Request for Debt Validation - [Account Number or Reference Number]

To Whom It May Concern:

I am writing in response to your [letter/call] received on [insert date], regarding an alleged debt you claim I owe. Under the Fair Debt Collection Practices Act (FDCPA), 15 U.S.C. § 1692g, I am requesting that you provide proper validation of this debt.

Please provide the following:

1. The name and address of the original creditor
2. The original amount of the debt and any interest or fees added
3. A copy of any agreement bearing my signature
4. Documentation proving that you are legally authorized to collect this debt
5. Proof that the debt is still within the statute of limitations for collection in my state

Until you provide this documentation, you are required to cease all collection activity, including reporting this debt to credit bureaus. If you have already reported this debt to any credit reporting agency, please notify them that the debt is currently being disputed.

DISPUTE LETTER TO CREDIT BUREAU

Your Name
Address
Home Phone
Work Phone

Name of Consumer Reporting Company
{Experian / TransUnion / CSC-Equifax / Innovis}
Street Address
City, State, Zip Code

RE: Social Security Number
Credit Report #

I have recently acquired my credit report. After carefully reviewing its contents, I have found some inaccurate information that needs to be updated.

I realize the importance to both parties of having an accurate credit report. Knowing this, please bring up to date the accounts listed on the enclosed document(s) under the provisions of the Fair Credit Reporting Act's (FCRA) 15 USC Section 1681i. According to the act...
"a period of thirty (30) days shall be 'reasonable time' to investigate and update the account(s) in question unless you notify me immediately otherwise."

Additionally, 15 USC Sections 1681i(d) and 1681j of the Fair Credit Reporting Act requires that I receive written notification of the updates, an up-to-date credit report (at no charge), and that an updated credit report be sent to anyone who received my credit report within the last six (6) months.

Please send me an updated report once all inaccurate accounts are removed or corrected. Please investigate the following accounts:

CREDITOR _____
ACCOUNT NUMBER _____
REASON: (Ex: Account was paid and not past due 120 days)

Thank you for your prompt attention to this matter.

Regards,
Print Name

FRAUD LETTER TO CREDITOR

Date
Your Name
Your Address
City, State, Zip Code
Your Account Number
Name of Creditor
Billing Inquiries
Address
City, State, Zip Code

Dear Sir or Madam:

I am writing to dispute a fraudulent (charge or debit) on my account in the amount of $_____. I am a victim of identity theft and I did not make this (charge or debit). I am requesting that the (charge be removed or the debit be reinstated), that any finance and other miscellaneous charges related to the fraudulent amount be credited, and that I receive an accurate and current statement depicting these corrections.

Enclosed are copies of my police report and identity theft affidavit, which outlines my previous statement. Please investigate this matter in a prompt manner and correct the fraudulent (charge or debit) as soon as possible.

Sincerely,
Your Name

Enclosures: (List what you are enclosing)

NO RESPONSE LETTER TO CREDIT BUREAU

NO RESPONSE LETTER TO CREDIT BUREAU

Your Name
Address
Home Phone Number

Name of Consumer Reporting Company
{Experian / TransUnion / CSC-Equifax / Innovis}
Address
City, State, Zip Code

RE: Social Security Number
Credit Report #

On [insert month/date/year], I sent a letter to your agency requesting an investigation and the removal of inaccurate information as it relates to my credit report [insert report #]. I requested that you respond within thirty (30) days, as the law states. However, I have not received notification or a reply from your agency regarding this matter.

Once again, please investigate the following accounts under the provisions of the Fair Credit Reporting Act (FCRA), 15 USC Section 1681i:
[list creditor] & [list account number];
[list creditor] & [list account number];
[list creditor] & [list account number];
and [list creditor] & [list account number].

The FCRA states, "A period of thirty (30) days shall be 'reasonable time' to investigate the accounts in question, unless you notify me immediately. Failure to verify the above information within the thirty (30) day time period constitutes "non-verification" and the accounts in question must be immediately removed from my credit file and credit report."

Additionally, 15 USC Sections 1681i(d) and 1681j of the FCRA require that I receive written notification of the updates, an updated credit report (at no charge), and that an up-to-date credit report be sent to the persons who received my credit report within the last six (6) months.

Should you have any questions or need further clarification, please contact me using the above contact information.

Thank you for your time and cooperation.

Sincerely,
Signature
Printed Name
Date

ADD CREDITOR LETTER

Your Name
Address
Home Phone
Work Phone
Social Security Number
Credit Report #

Name of Consumer Reporting Company
{Experian / TransUnion / CSC-Equifax / Innovis}
Address
City, State, Zip Code

RE: Social Security Number
Credit Report #

I have recently acquired my credit report [insert credit report # here] and after carefully reviewing its contents, I have found that there are some accounts that currently are not being reported. It is my feeling that the accounts that are not being reported should be included in my credit report. I am requesting to add the following accounts to my credit report:

Creditor _____ Acct # _____
Creditor _____ Acct # _____
Creditor _____ Acct # _____
Creditor _____ Acct # _____

Please refer to the attached documentation supporting the fact that the above stated accounts do indeed belong to me and are currently in good standing.

The Fair Credit Reporting Act (FCRA) and 15 USC Section 1681 (b) states,
'It is the purpose of this title (FCRA) to require that the consumer reporting agencies adopt reasonable procedures for meeting the needs of commerce for consumer credit, personnel, insurance, and other related information in a timely manner which is fair and equitable to the consumer, with regard to the confidentiality, accuracy, relevancy, and proper utilization of such information in accordance with the requirements of this title.'

According to the FCRA, it is the credit reporting agency's responsibility to add the accounts listed above to my personal credit file. Please update my credit report by adding the additional accounts listed as requested to my trades and payments histories.

Should you have any questions or need further clarification, please contact me using the above contact information.

Thank you for your time and cooperation.

Sincerely,
Name: (print)
Signature:
Date:

CEASE AND DESIST LETTER

[Your Name]
[Your Address]
[City, State, ZIP Code]
[Email Address]
[Phone Number]

[Date]

[Debt Collector's Name]
[Debt Collector's Address]
[City, State, ZIP Code]

RE: Cease and Desist - Continued Collection Efforts on Disputed Debt
Account Number: [Insert Account or Reference Number]

To Whom It May Concern:

This letter serves as a formal notice under the Fair Debt Collection Practices Act (FDCPA), 15 U.S.C. § 1692c(c), instructing you to cease all collection activities regarding the alleged debt referenced above.

I previously submitted a written debt validation request on [insert date] in response to your initial communication dated [insert date of first contact]. As of today, I have not received sufficient validation or verification of this alleged debt as required under 15 U.S.C. § 1692g(b).

Despite this, your agency has continued to engage in collection activities, including [insert applicable violations such as phone calls, letters, or reporting to credit bureaus], which is a direct violation of federal law.

I now demand that you:
1. Immediately cease all collection efforts, including phone calls, letters, and credit reporting
2. Provide written confirmation that no further action will be taken
3. Remove any reporting to credit bureaus related to this disputed debt

IDENTITY THEFT DISPUTE LETTER

Date
Name
Address
City, State, Zip Code
Phone Number
Email Address

Company Name or Credit Bureau
Company Address
City, State, Zip Code

Subject: Identity Theft Victim – Dispute of Fraudulent Account Information

Dear [Company or Credit Bureau Name],

I am writing to notify you that I am the victim of identity theft. I recently discovered that fraudulent accounts and/or charges have been made using my personal information without my permission.

The following account(s) or item(s) on my credit report are fraudulent and were not authorized by me:
- Account Name: [Name of Creditor or Company]
- Account Number: [Account Number]
- Amount: [Balance or Amount in Dispute]

Under the Fair Credit Reporting Act (FCRA), I am requesting that you immediately block the fraudulent information from appearing on my credit report and cease all collection activity related to the unauthorized account(s).

I have attached a copy of my Identity Theft Report (such as a report filed with the Federal Trade Commission or local law enforcement) and copies of documents verifying my identity, including a government-issued photo ID and proof of residence.

Please investigate this matter and confirm removal of the fraudulent information in writing. I also request that you provide a copy of my updated credit report reflecting these changes.

Thank you for your prompt attention to this serious matter. If you require any additional information from me to process this dispute, please contact me at [phone number] or [email address].

Sincerely,
Name and Signature

Attachments:
- Copy of Identity Theft Report (police report or FTC report)
- Copy of government-issued ID (driver's license, passport)
- Proof of address (utility bill, bank statement, etc.)

IDENTITY THEFT AFFIDAVIT

IDENTITY THEFT AFFIDAVIT

Victim Information
Full Name: _____
Address: _____
City, State, ZIP: _____
Phone: _____
Email: _____
Date of Birth: _____
SSN (last 4 digits): _____

Incident Description
Briefly describe the identity theft incident:
_____
_____

Fraudulent Accounts
List known fraudulent accounts (account # and institution):
_____
_____

Law Enforcement Report
Report Number: _____
Police Department: _____
Phone: _____
Officer's Name: _____

Declaration
I certify that the information provided is accurate to the best of my knowledge.
Signature: _____ Date: _____

Notary Section
State of _____
County of _____
Sworn and subscribed before me this ____ day of _____, 20__
Notary Public Signature: _____
My Commission Expires: _____

IDENTITY THEFT AFFIDAVIT INSTRUCTIONS
1. Complete this affidavit in as much detail as possible.
2. Attach a copy of a government-issued photo ID (e.g., driver's license, passport).
3. Include documents related to the identity theft (e.g., police report, credit report).
4. Sign and date the affidavit in the presence of a notary public.
5. Submit the completed affidavit to the requesting organization (e.g., credit bureau, lender).

Financial Terms Glossary

— A —

Adjustable-Rate Mortgage (ARM)

A mortgage that features predetermined adjustments of the loan interest rate at regular intervals based on an established index. The interest rate is adjusted at each interval to a rate equivalent to the index value, plus a predetermined spread or margin, over the index, and usually subjected to per-interval and to life-to-loan interest rate and/ or payment rate caps.

Advantage Score

Scoring System developed by the three (3) credit bureaus to replace FICO scoring.

Amortization

The repayment of a loan by installments.

Annual Fee

A yearly fee charged by the credit grantors for the privilege of using a credit card.

Annual Percentage Rate (APR)

The periodic rate times the number of periods in a year. (For example: A 5% quarterly return has an APR of 20%.)

Applicant

A person applying for credit privileges, employment, or other benefits.

Assets

Every form of property owned by a debtor.

Authorized Account User

The person that is authorized by the contractually responsible party to use the account.

Automatic Stay

The restricting of liability holders from collection efforts related to collateral seizure. This is automatically imposed when a firm files for bankruptcy under Chapter 7, 11, and 13.

— B —

Bankruptcy

A proceeding in the United States Federal Court that may legally release a person from repaying debts owed. The law contains several *chapters* which relate to various methods of relief:

Chapter 7 - Straight Bankruptcy (Total Liquidation of Assets)

Chapter 11 - Business Reorganization

Chapter 12 - Farm Debt Bankruptcy

Chapter 13 - Wage Earner Repayment Plan

Bankruptcy Chapter 7

This is a type of bankruptcy in which the debtor's assets are liquidated to satisfy a person's credit obligations, which are then removed at the conclusion of the bankruptcy.

Bankruptcy Chapter 13

This type of bankruptcy allows a person to retain assets in exchange for making reduced payments in

accordance to a trustee-approved plan.

Bankruptcy Discharge

A court order terminating the bankruptcy proceedings on old debts.

Bankruptcy Dismissal

A court order that denies one's bankruptcy petition, therefore making the debtor still liable for all debts.

Budget

A financial plan for saving and spending currency.

— C —

Charge Card

A card that requires payment in full upon the receipt of the statement.

Charge Card

Accounting term that is used to indicate that the creditor does not expect to collect a balance owed on the account.

Charge-Off

Occurs when a creditor writes off a debt as a loss after the borrower has become seriously delinquent, typically after 180 days (or about six months) of non-payment.

Collateral

An item of value that guarantees payment of debt or may be collected in the replacement of a payment.

Collection Account

Refers to the status of an account owed to a creditor when the account has been transferred from a routine debt to a collections department of the creditor's firm or to a separate professional debt collection firm.

Collection Agency

A third party agency that creditors use to collect debt. A collection agency is also a company that is

established by a creditor to collect a debt, which is also referred to as a credit agency.

Consolidated Loan

A loan usually obtained for the purpose of reducing the amount of the payments for the bills owed by consolidating the sum total of the bills into one loan payment amount. The consumer pays off several bills with the proceeds from one loan and is left with one consolidated monthly payment.

Consumer

Person who uses and/or purchases goods and services for family or personal use.

Consumer Credit Counseling (CCA)

Organizations that help consumers find various avenues to repay debts owed through careful budgeting and management of funds. These are usually non-profit organizations that are funded by creditors. By requesting that the creditors accept a longer pay-off period, the counseling services can often construct a successful repayment plan.

Consumer Report

Also known as a credit report, a factual record of an individual's credit payment history. Its main purpose is to assist a lender more efficiently and objectively decide whether to give the consumer applicable credit. A consumer report is used to develop a credit score, but does not contain an actual numerical score.

Consumer Reporting Agencies (CRA)

Companies that gather and sell information regarding where a consumer works and lives, how to pay their bills, and whether they've been sued, arrested, or have filed for bankruptcy. The most common type of CRA is a credit bureau. The information that CRA's sell concerning the consumer to creditors, employers, insurers, and other businesses is called a Consumer Report or a Credit Report.

Cosigner

A person that officially undertakes the responsibility for a loan in the event of the borrower's default.

Credit

A trust or promise to pay for goods and services at a later date or time, while purchasing the items or services at the exact or current moment.

Credit Agency

Third party agency creditors that are utilized to collect debt. Often times, a credit agency is a company that is established by the creditor with the task of collecting debt. which may also be referred to as a collection agency.

Credit Bureau

Private, for-profit companies that compile information about a consumer's credit history and sell the information to banks, credit card companies, landlords, employers, and other interested parties.

Credit Card

Usually a rectangular piece of plastic that is encoded and encrypted with a consumer's financial information, used in the place of cash currency or checks, which authorizes the purchase payment for goods and services.

Credit Counseling Service

Companies that provide debt management plans and budget counseling, usually in return for a given fee.

Credit Grantor

An individual or business furnishing consumer goods and/or services on credit.

Credit Limit

The maximum amount of funds that you can charge on a particular credit account.

Credit History

A record based on information supplied over time by creditors with whom consumers have conducted business transactions. This information is reflected in a credit report.

Creditor

An individual or business who extends credit and to whom the funds are owed.

Credit Repair Companies

Individuals or companies that promise to "clean up" or "erase" a consumer's bad credit and give them a fresh start to financial freedom. Credit Repair Companies are also known as Credit Clinics.

Credit Report

Also referred to as a Consumer Report, the document is a factual record of an individual's credit payment history. Its main purpose is to assist a lender in efficiently and objectively decide whether to grant a consumer the credit that is being requested or that is applicable. A credit report is used to develop a consumer's credit score, but does not contain a numerical score.

Credit Score

A numerical value that provides a representation of a consumer's credit at a given point in time. Credit scores are calculated using data contained in a consumer's credit report. The score assesses the likelihood that a borrower will repay a loan or the credit that is being issued.

Credit Utilization Ratio

The percentage of your available credit that you currently use. It is calculated by dividing your total credit balances by your total credit limits and multiplying by 100. Credit utilization is one of the most important factors in your credit score typically, it's recommended to keep your utilization below 30% to maintain or improve your score.

— *D* —

Debit Card

Usually a rectangular piece of plastic that is encrypted or encoded with the consumer's financial information. in which funds used towards purchase transactions are deducted directly from the consumer's personal checking or savings account.

Debt Load

The total amount of funds that a consumer owes.

Debt Management Plan

A plan that assists consumers to effectively repay their debt and helps creditors collect the funds owed them. This document is usually provided by a Credit Counseling Agency.

Debt-to-Income Ratio (DTI)

measures the percentage of your monthly gross income that goes toward paying your monthly debt obligations.

It is calculated by dividing your total monthly debt payments by your gross monthly income (before taxes) and multiplying by 100.

Lenders use DTI to assess your ability to manage monthly payments and repay debts. A lower DTI shows that you have a good balance between debt and income, while a higher DTI may make it harder to qualify for new loans or credit.

Debtor

An individual who uses credit cards, owes funds towards a personal loan, or is paying out funds on a home mortgage or business transaction.

Debt Collector

An individual who regularly collects debts owed to other entities. This includes attorneys who collect debt on a regular basis.

Debt-to-Income Ratio (DTI)

Measures the percentage of your monthly gross income that goes toward paying your monthly debt obligations.

It is calculated by dividing your total monthly debt payments by your gross monthly income (before taxes) and multiplying by 100.

Lenders use DTI to assess your ability to manage monthly payments and repay debts. A lower DTI shows that you have a good balance between debt and income, while a higher DTI may make it harder to qualify for new loans or credit.

Default

Occurs when a borrower fails to repay a debt obligation in accordance with the specified terms of an agreement, contract, or payment arrangement.

Dischargeable Debt

Debt that can be eliminated in the process of bankruptcy.

— E —

Equal Credit Opportunity Act (ECOA)

A federal law that requires lenders and other creditors to make credit equally available without discrimination based on race, ethnicity, religion, national origin, age, sex, marital status, or receipt of income from public assistance programs.

Equifax/CSC

One of the four (4) major credit-reporting agencies.

Experian

One of the four (4) major credit-reporting agencies.

— F —

FICO Score/Scoring

A credit score developed by the Fair Isaac & Co. Credit, in which the scoring determines the likelihood that a person will pay their bills. The score is calculated by using scoring models and mathematical tables that assign points for different pieces of information which best predict future credit performances.

Fair Credit Reporting Act (FCRA)

A federal law that was established in 1971 and revised in 1997, which enables consumers to learn pertinent information that the Credit Reporting Agencies have on file about them, and to dispute inaccurate data in the file. It also establishes specific permissible purposes for which credit reports may be requested; time limits may also be placed on how long adverse information may be reported.

Fair Debt Collections Practice Act (FDCPA)

An act that requires debt collectors to treat the consumer fairly and prohibit certain methods of debt collecting. For example, you can ask a collector not to ever call you and also address your request in a letter. By following these actions, the debt collector is no longer allowed to call you. If the debt collector does not abide by your request, any continued calls made to you will be against the laws of the FDCPA, in which the debt collection company can be sued.

— G —

Garnishment

Legal process whereas a creditor has obtained judgment on a debt and may obtain full or partial payment by seizure of a portion of the debtor's assets. (Wages, bank accounts, etc.)

Grace Period

The period of time allowed to avoid any finance penalty charges by paying off the balance in full before the due date of the applicable credit that is used or obtained.

— H —

Hard Inquiry

(Also called a hard pull) occurs when a lender or creditor checks your credit report as part of a lending decision, such as applying for a credit card, auto loan, mortgage, or apartment lease.

Hard inquiries may cause a small, temporary drop in your credit score, typically by a few points. Multiple hard inquiries in a short period can have a bigger impact, especially if they are for different types of credit.

However, when you are shopping for a loan (like a mortgage or car loan), multiple inquiries within a short time frame (usually 14–45 days, depending on the scoring model) are typically counted as a single inquiry to minimize the impact.

Financial Terms Glossary

Home Equity Loan

A loan based on the difference of the amount you own on your home and the home's current market value.

— I —

Innovis

One of the Four (4) major credit-reporting agencies

Inquiry

A request made by the creditors to view a consumer's credit report.

Installment Loan

A credit account in which the amount of the payment and the number of payments are predetermined or fixed.

Interest

The percentage that a creditor charges on funds borrowed.

— J —

Judgment

The official court decision of an action or suit. This public record may be listed on your credit report in matters pertaining to funds and/or debts owed.

— L —

Lawsuit

A legal action that is taken against an individual or entity for the purpose of receiving a judgment.

Lease

A written document containing the conditions under which the possession and use of real and/or personal property are given by the owner to another party for a determined period and for a stated consideration.

LexisNexis

A database that gathers public records and financial data often used by lenders, insurers, and debt collectors. It can include information not listed on your standard credit report such as eviction records or insurance claims.

Lien

A legal hold or claim of an individual on the property of another as security for a debt or charge. The right given by law to satisfy debt. (A lien must be paid and released.]

Loan

An arrangement whereby a creditor gives a company or individual specified funds and arranges for the funds to be repaid within a specified timeline. Most loans are usually repaid with a calculated amount of interest.

— M —

Minimum Payment

The smallest amount you are required to pay on a credit card balance to keep the account in good standing.

Mortgage

A lien or claim against real property given by the buyer to the lender as security for funds borrowed.

1st Mortgage - Also known as the "primary" mortgage in which it as priority over the claims of subsequent lenders for the same property.

2nd Mortgage - Also known as the "secondary" mortgage that is a loan secured by a mortgage or trust deed, in which the lien is "junior" to another mortgage or trust.

Middle Score

The average FICO score that is calculated between all three (3) major credit bureaus.

For example, the average score for Experian is 650, TransUnion is 710, and Equifax-CSC is 700. Thus, the average middle score would calculate to 686.

Minimum Payment

The smallest amount you must pay on a credit card balance to keep the account in good standing. If the book discusses making at least the minimum payment, include this term in the glossary with a note that paying only the minimum leads to high interest costs over time.

— N —

Non-Dischargeable Debt

A debt that cannot be eliminated through the process of bankruptcy.

A legal action that is taken against an individual or entity for the purpose of receiving a judgment.

— P —

Permissible Purpose

As defined in Section 604 of the Fair Credit Reporting Act, only the named reasons for requesting a credit report are deemed "permissible". Requests not meeting these criteria must be denied.

Personal Lines of Credit

The maximum amount you can owe at any time based on your income, debt, and your credit history.

Personal Loan

A loan based on the criteria of your income, debt, and credit history.

Petition

A written document that initiates a bankruptcy case procedure.

Principal

The outstanding balance of a loan, exclusive of interest and other miscellaneous charges.

Public Record

Information that is obtained by the Credit Reporting Agency derived from court records such as liens, bankruptcy filings, and judgments. Public records are open to any person who requests to see them.

— R —

Repossession

Forced or voluntary surrender of merchandise or property as a result of the customer's failure to pay or comply with the terms of an agreement as initially promised. There are several types and descriptions of repossession actions.

Revolving Account

An account that requires at least a specified minimum monthly payment, plus an additional service charge to the balance. As the balance declines, the amount of the service charge or interest also declines.

Revolving Credit

A type of credit that allows you to borrow, repay, and then borrow again up to a set credit limit.

You are not required to pay off the full balance each month, but you must make at least a minimum payment. Interest is charged on any unpaid balance.

— S —

Financial Terms Glossary

Secured Credit Card

A credit card that is provided after a consumer deposits funds into an account. Charges may only be made up to the amount deposited.

Secured Debt

A type of loan or credit that is backed by collateral — something of value that the lender can claim if the borrower fails to repay the debt.

Common examples of secured debt include mortgages (backed by your home) and auto loans (backed by your vehicle).

Because the lender has the right to seize the collateral if you default, secured debts often come with lower interest rates compared to unsecured debts.

Secured Debt Card

Debts linked to collateral. The collateral guarantees payment of the debt or the creditor has the right to take the collateral. Secured debt is most commonly used when purchasing homes or automobiles.

Secured Personal Loan

A loan in which the funds are provided after a consumer deposits funds into an account. Charges may only be made up to the amount deposited.

Smart Card

An electronic prepaid cash card usually sold at a bank, that is used at face value in exchange for goods and/or services.

Soft Inquiry

(Also called a **soft pull**) happens when your credit report is checked, but not because you applied for new credit.

Examples include when you check your own credit, when a lender pre-approves you for an offer, or when an employer checks your credit as part of a background screening (with your permission).

Soft inquiries **do not affect your credit score** and may or may not appear on credit reports viewed by lenders.

— T —

TransUnion

One of the four (4) major credit-reporting agencies.

Trustee

A trustee is appointed in Chapter 7 and Chapter 13 bankruptcy cases to review the debtor's schedules, manage payments, and generally represent the interests of the creditors in the bankruptcy case. The role of the trustee is different under the various bankruptcy chapters.

— U —

Unsecured Debt

Debt with no collateral. Commonly used with credit cards, medical bills, student loans, rent, and personal loans from friends or family.

References

Credit Reporting Agencies:
- Experian. (n.d.). Experian Credit Reports and Scores. Retrieved from https://www.experian.com
- Equifax. (n.d.). Equifax Consumer Services. Retrieved from https://www.equifax.com
- TransUnion. (n.d.). TransUnion Consumer Solutions. Retrieved from https://www.transunion.com
- Innovis. (n.d.). Innovis Consumer Assistance. Retrieved from https://www.innovis.com

Federal Laws and Regulations:
- Fair Credit Reporting Act (FCRA), 15 U.S. Code § 1681.
- Federal Trade Commission (FTC). (n.d.). Consumer Rights Under the FCRA. Retrieved from https://www.ftc.gov
- Consumer Financial Protection Bureau (CFPB). (n.d.). Know Your Rights Under the FCRA. Retrieved from https://www.consumerfinance.gov

Consumer Data and Analytics:
- LexisNexis Risk Solutions. (n.d.). Consumer Disclosure Reports. Retrieved from https://consumer.risk.lexisnexis.com

Annual Credit Reports:
- AnnualCreditReport.com. (n.d.). Free Annual Credit Reports. Retrieved from https://www.annualcreditreport.com

Scriptural References:
- The Holy Bible, New King James Version (NKJV).
Hosea 4:6 — "My people are destroyed for lack of knowledge..."
Ecclesiastes 7:1 — "A good name is better than precious ointment..."

www.ingramcontent.com/pod-product-compliance
Lightning Source LLC
Chambersburg PA
CBHW060829050426
42453CB00008B/632